CW01640880

Provincial House Restoration

The National and Provincial Guide to House Restoration

National & Provincial Building Society

Kogan Page

The masculine pronoun has been used throughout this book. This stems from a desire to avoid ugly and cumbersome language, and no discrimination, prejudice or bias is intended.

To the best knowledge of the Publisher and the National and Provincial Building Society all the information in this book is correct at the time of going to press. Neither party, however, can be held responsible for any inaccuracies that may occur.

© Kogan Page 1989

All rights reserved. No reproduction, copy or transmission of this publication may be made without written permission.

No paragraph of this publication may be reproduced, copied or transmitted save with written permission or in accordance with the provisions of the Copyright Act 1956 (as amended), or under the terms of any licence permitting limited copying issued by the Copyright Licensing Agency, 7 Ridgmount Street, London WC1E 7AE.

Any person who does any unauthorised act in relation to this publication may be liable to criminal prosecution and civil claims for damages.

First published in 1989 by
Kogan Page Ltd,
120 Pentonville Rd, London N1 9JN
in association with the National and Provincial Building Society,
Provincial House, Bradford BD1 1NL.

Typeset by DP Photosetting, Aylesbury, Bucks
Printed and bound in Great Britain by

British Library Cataloguing in Publication Data
The National & Provincial guide to house restoration
1. Great Britain. Houses. Restoration
I. Title
728.3′028′8

ISBN 07494-0053-6

Contents

Preface

Buying a run-down property to restore presents many of us with an exciting opportunity to fulfil our ambition to create a dream home. At the National and Provincial Building Society we are committed to improving and extending our range of products and services to meet the needs of our customers. By talking to many of you we have recognised that finding a lender who is flexible enough to support you in your plans to renovate a property in disrepair can often be difficult, expensive and discouraging! With this problem in mind we have developed our House Restoration Mortgage.

The House Restoration Mortgage is best described as a package which combines flexible finance with advice and support throughout the restoration of your property. This book, which forms part of the restoration package, intends to provide you with practical tips and guidance to help you successfully implement your plans whatever the scale of work envisaged. We hope you find it useful.

Happy Renovating!

Bob Larkham
Director of Mortgages

Acknowledgements

The National and Provincial Building Society and Kogan Page would like to thank the following people for their contributions to this book: Bob Buchanan, Howard Green, Kim Ludman and Penelope Woolf.

PART 1

OBTAINING THE PROPERTY

1
What Can This Book Do For Me?

The thought of buying a run-down property and turning it into a dream house is one that many of us are likely to have had at some stage. Restoring an older property is certainly an exciting challenge and can be very rewarding. It is, however, a process that requires careful planning right from the start.

This book is written for the layman and aims to demystify the restoration process by explaining in straightforward terms how to go about selecting a property and financing and managing its restoration. The book assumes no previous experience and no professional knowledge. It is not written for the architect, builder or surveyor but for the ordinary home-owner who wants to know how to use his own skills and those of professionals to the best advantage at the least cost.

Whether you intend to move straight into your newly-acquired property and restore it gradually or whether you decide to have all the work carried out before you move in must be your choice, and will be determined by your individual needs and circumstances. This book covers both eventualities. It is intended to guide you in the restoration of your property whatever the scale of work required.

Included in the word 'restoration' are the following terms:

- Renovation
- Conversion
- Maintenance
- Repairs
- Improvements
- Additions.

The work could range from repairing roof slates and installing a damp proof course to the conversion of a windmill into a family home.

Some people may choose to carry out the work themselves; others will prefer to hire professionals such as architects, surveyors or qualified tradesmen. It may be advantageous for you to carry out some of the work yourself and to rely on professionals for more difficult tasks. Again, this book covers all these options and can be used so that you can work out a programme tailored to fit your individual needs.

What does the book cover?

All stages of the restoration process are covered step by step. This book will lead you through the sequence of:

Obtaining finance

↓

Finding a property

↓

Buying the property

↓

Planning for renovation

↓

Deciding how much to do yourself

↓

Knowing what to do if things go wrong.

It includes details of the various professional and trade associations and descriptions of the codes of practice to which their members are obliged to conform. Useful addresses provide a reliable source of information enabling you to contact a suitably qualified professional and allowing you to make a complaint should his work turn out to be less than satisfactory.

2
Money Matters

Assuming that you intend to buy a property to restore, you will have to consider not only how to cover the cost of the restoration work but also how to finance the purchase. It is advisable that you have your finances worked out *before* you begin to look for a property. An informal chat with your building society at this stage will help you to establish your budget. Once you have a clear idea of what you can afford, and how you are going to raise the money, you will be in a better position to begin house hunting. The alternative, selecting a property first and then thinking whether you can afford it, can lead to disappointment. This chapter outlines the various sources of finance on offer and the different ways in which the restoration work can be funded.

Sources of finance

Your own money, family and friends

Few people are likely to be able to afford to buy and restore a property without having to borrow money to finance the project. Borrowing from family or friends is a possibility but they are unlikely to want to tie up, for an indefinite period of time, any extra money they might have. Parents will often help their children to get started on the property ladder by lending them some money towards the deposit they must normally put down on the property. Most people, however, will not be able to raise money through family and friends and will be dependent on a mortgage.

Mortgages and other loans

Everyone is familiar with the idea of approaching a building society for a mortgage to suit their individual needs. A new development is the introduction of a *House Restoration Mortgage* which is currently offered only by the National and Provincial Building Society. This is a mortgage which has been specially developed for those people who are looking for a property to buy and restore. This mortgage provides you with the finance to buy a property and also enables you to carry out repairs and improvements as part of the mortgage.

A House Restoration Mortgage works on the principle that as you carry out work on the property so it increases in value. You will have already agreed with the building society how much money will be released as each stage of your programme is completed. The advantage is that you can increase your mortgage as the work progresses and you do not have to pay interest on money that you are not using.

Whether a House Restoration Mortgage or a traditional mortgage, combined perhaps with a home improvement loan, is most suitable for you will depend on your own particular circumstances. Your building society can advise you about the options available and about the best way to finance your plans at the least cost to yourself.

A mortgage is an example of a *secured loan*. A secured loan is where the borrower normally wishes to raise a large sum of money and the lender therefore requires something of value to support such a significant outlay. The item of value is known as collateral. In the case of a mortgage, the collateral will be your property. The fact that you are able to offer the lender some collateral means that his risk is reduced and therefore that the interest you will be charged on the borrowed sum will be less than the rate you would pay if the loan were unsecured. You will usually find that a secured loan has a longer repayment term (ie 20–25 years for a mortgage), although this can vary.

An *unsecured loan*, as it suggests, is not supported by collateral and represents an increased risk to the lender. You would therefore expect to pay a higher rate of interest on this type of loan. An unsecured loan would usually be the choice for short-term borrowing (ie up to five years).

Two examples of unsecured loans are an *overdraft* and a *personal loan.* An overdraft facility may be arranged on your bank current account. This allows you to go into debt up to a pre-arranged limit. The benefit of an overdraft is that you pay interest only on the amount of money that you are using at any one time. However, interest rates vary from one lending institution to another, and you are advised to shop around to ensure that you do not end up paying excessive interest charges. During the period of the overdraft, interest rates may fluctuate and this will be reflected in the amount of interest you pay.

A personal loan can be arranged through your building society or bank. The interest rate is likely to be fixed for the period of the loan, which gives you the benefit of a known repayment sum. However, you are charged interest on the full amount of the loan from the start irrespective of whether or not you spend it straight away.

Choosing between a secured and an unsecured loan is something that you must decide as it depends on your individual circumstances and on the nature of the property you intend to buy and restore. It is important, therefore, to discuss your needs with a reputable lender such as a building society whose staff can offer expert advice free of charge.

Home Improvement Grants

It is always worth investigating whether you are eligible for a grant towards house restoration. Grants are awarded by the local authority and your eligibility for one is affected by where you live. The four types of grant are discussed briefly below. If you think you might be eligible for a grant then you should contact the Improvement Grant Officer at your local authority for a leaflet which explains the grants in more detail. Although the grants are standard, the rules governing them will vary from one local authority to another. Details about the various grants given below will not be the same in all parts of the country, so do check locally to see which rules apply to you.

Intermediate grant

This grant is available for houses built before 1901 and concerns provision for basic amenities. It is a mandatory grant which means that you have the right to it if you satisfy certain basic conditions. These are if your property lacks a:

- Bathroom or shower
- Handbasin
- Sink
- Water closet
- Supply of cold or hot water to any of the above amenities and has not had any of these before.

In addition, certain other associated works also qualify: for example drainage, repairs and decorations, other installation of some or all of the above, alterations to gas, electricity or water services to allow any of the above to be installed and essential repairs. The grant is payable as a percentage based on certain price limits. The sum available is for 75 per cent of the approved works, or 90 per cent in cases of hardship.

Improvement grant
This grant is usually available for houses built before 1 January 1919, except in some cases where the date is 2 October 1961. Generally, 50 per cent of the work carried out must be 'improvements'. Repairs do qualify but usually only where they support the improvements. The local Improvement Grant Officer will advise you on what constitutes an 'improvement'.

After the work is completed the property will have to conform to the following standards. It will need to:

- Be substantially free from damp
- Have adequate natural lighting and ventilation
- Have adequate and safe provision throughout for artificial lighting and have sufficient electric socket outlets for the safe and proper functioning of domestic appliances
- Be provided with adequate drainage facilities
- Be in a stable structural condition
- Have satisfactory internal arrangements
- Have satisfactory facilities for preparing and cooking food
- Be provided with adequate facilities for heating
- Have adequate provision for the storage of fuel (where necessary) and for the storage of refuse
- Have space thermal insulation in the roof sufficient to give for the relevant structure a 'U' value of $0.35W/m^2°C$. (U value defines

how much heat will pass through a material — the lower the figure the more heat is stored.)

Repair grant
To be eligible for this grant, your house must predate 1 January 1919. Repairs must be structural and have a minimum value of £2,400. The rateable value of the property must be more than £226 (£400 in Greater London). The grant that you are awarded is based on a percentage of the maximum eligible expense limit of £4,800. The sum available is 75 per cent of the value of the work as a grant and 90 per cent in cases of hardship. Work usually covered will include:

- Roofs — repairing and replacing defective roofs and timbers
- External walls — renewing or repairing defective walls, doors, windows and damp proof course
- Foundations — repair or renewal or underpinning
- Floors — repair or replacement
- Internal works — repair or replacement of walls, ceilings or staircases.

Special grant
Owners of houses that have been converted into flats, where tenants are not members of the family but are sharing facilities, may be entitled to a special grant for the provision of separate basic amenities. Fire escapes can also be funded by this grant together with any repairs that will be necessary. This is a discretionary grant (awarded at the discretion of the local authority) but becomes mandatory if the council has served you with a notice under Section 352 of the Housing Act 1985 (as amended by the Housing Act 1988). In either case, the grant would be 75 per cent (20 per cent in Greater London) of the approved cost of the works (90 per cent in cases of hardship excluding Greater London), up to £10,500 (£14,000 in Greater London) for the means of escape from fire, and £3,400 for associated repairs (£4,800 in Greater London).

• • • • •

Special rates apply on all grants for disabled people. Furthermore, if you live in a listed building you may be eligible for greater sums. In either case, you should consult your local authority for advice. It is important to remember that you must not begin work until the grant has been awarded. Some local authorities will also make it a condition that the property is not sold for five years. Others may require you to pay a proportion of the grant back if you sell the property within a certain time, so always check the conditions on which the grant is awarded.

Now that you have given careful consideration to money matters you can begin to look for a property that you are confident you will have the finances to buy and renovate.

3
Finding a Property

As buying a property is likely to be the biggest investment you make, your choice is critical. Before setting out to find a property to buy and restore it is useful to give careful consideration to your needs. Your 'finding campaign' will need to be well thought out and carefully executed.

The sort of property that you view will depend on your motives for wanting to buy and renovate it. This book assumes that your main motive is to provide yourself and your family with a stable, attractive house in which you will live for at least the next few years. Whatever your motives, you are advised to consider your basic requirements.

What are my basic requirements?

It is very important when you are house hunting to have an idea of your requirements as it is all too easy to get carried away and make the wrong decision. Do not let anyone rush you or put pressure on you to make a hasty decision.

If you ignore your needs you can rush headlong into the purchase of a property which is totally inappropriate for you. Attractive as that small cottage may be, it is no good falling in love with it, forgetting that you will soon be needing an extra bedroom and that, because it is in a National Park, you are unlikely to be granted permission to extend it. The advantages of a property are all too clear to see and you must discipline yourself so that you also consider its disadvantages. A house covered in ivy may look idyllic but what would it be like to live in? Would it be riddled with damp? Train yourself to consider the negative as well as the positive features of every property you look at.

Preparing a list of what you are looking for in your next home is useful and can be used each time you visit a house or flat. Give some thought to your plans for the next few years. This will enable you to focus on both your short-term and longer-term needs. The checklist on page 22 will help you to think about your own requirements. It covers wide-ranging considerations like starting a family to the detail of how many sockets you would like in each room. This is not an exhaustive list but should be used to enable you to design your own 'shopping list' for house hunting.

The source of heating is worth considering. If you have central heating in your present home and are convinced of its merits, do not forget to budget for the installation of central heating in your new house if it is without it.

Having made a list of your basic requirements and assessed your priorities, you can turn to the type of property you want to buy and renovate.

What type of property should I buy?

The restoration process can range from installing a damp proof course in a mid-terrace property to converting a barn. It is therefore helpful, when considering what sort of property to buy, to consider your motives as these will influence the nature of the restoration programme. As this book is written primarily for the householder who is restoring a property for his own use rather than for sale for profit, then it is likely that the restoration programme will not concentrate primarily on maximising profitability but will encompass individual preferences. For instance, solid oak designer kitchen units may cost you more than the value they add to your property, but on choosing to install them you will have considered how long you intend to live in the property and whether the enjoyment you get from them outweighs the extra cost.

Checklist

- Are you likely to start a family or have more children in the next few years? If so, you will need extra space.
- Will your children be leaving home? If so, it may be advisable to buy a smaller property.
- Will you require a study for occasions when you need to work from home?
- Will you want an extra room to use for friends and relatives when they visit you?
- Are elderly parents likely to come and live with you? If so, you may want to buy a property with enough land to enable you to add a 'granny flat'.
- Do you need a garage? If the answer is 'yes', how many cars must it be able to accommodate?
- Would you consider on-street parking? (Remember that this may affect the insurance cost of your car.)
- Is there room for you to park a boat/caravan/van?
- Would you take a property without a garden?
- Look out for the:
  - — number and distribution of electric power points or where these might be installed
  - — position of doors
  - — position, orientation and size of windows
  - — relationship of the rooms, for example the distance from the kitchen to the dining room
  - — source of heating
  - — layout of the property, for example whether you would have to walk through a bedroom to get to the only bathroom.

The type of property you buy will also be determined by the scale of work you are prepared to carry out. If you are happy to find alternative accommodation while a house is completely redesigned and rebuilt, and do not mind waiting a year before seeing the results, then your choice will obviously be wider! If, however, you intend to move in immediately you must either be prepared to suffer a little hardship or you must not opt for a house that needs extensive restoration.

A few people will choose to convert buildings currently used for other purposes. These include:

- Barns
- Mills
- Churches
- Schools
- Railway buildings
- Toll houses
- Gatekeepers' cottages
- Mews properties
- Castles.

More commonly, however, your choice will be between a:

- Terraced house
- Semi-detached house
- Detached house
- Bungalow
- Flat
- Maisonette.

Your choice of one of the above properties will be affected not only by your preference for that type of building and how much work needs to be done on it but also by your budget and your choice of where to live.

How much can I afford to spend on restoration work?

Reference was made in Chapter 2 to the various ways of financing the purchase and restoration of a property. The sort of property you choose will be limited by your budget and how much work you are prepared to put into the restoration programme. Remember that besides the purchase of the house and the cost of repairs and improvements you will also have to find money for:

- Solicitors' fees
- Professionals' fees, eg architects, surveyors
- Builders' and contractors' fees
- Stamp duty
- Unexpected costs.

It is essential, when planning your budget, to set aside money to cover any unexpected costs, as these will always arise and you should be prepared for them.

Where do I want to live?

There are many factors to take into account when you are deciding where to live. It is up to you to consider what is most important for you and your family and to weigh up the pros and cons of rural and urban lifestyles. You may have to make a compromise over some factors — the house of your choice may be very handy for the kids' school but you may have to commute a long way to work. It is important to be clear, at the outset, what your priorities are so that you can make informed choices.

You may already have a clear idea of where you want to live. You could, however, be considering moving to a different part of the country, in which case it is advisable to familiarise yourself with the different areas so that you get a better feel for the neighbourhood. Talking to local people or driving around urban areas at different times of day will give you valuable insights into whether or not you could live there.

Once the decision as to which areas you would like to buy in has been taken, you need information about properties for sale.

Where should I go for information on the availability of property?

Sources of information on property for sale include:

- Estate agents
- The press
- Friends and colleagues
- 'For sale' boards.

Estate agents

If you intend to carry out only minor work on a property then you do not need to single out buildings in need of restoration. If, however, you want to pick up a cheap property and renovate it yourself then tell the estate agent. He should be very responsive to this idea which will put you in a strong bargaining position as you may be ridding him of a property that he is having trouble selling. The estate agent will also be able to give you details about property for auction (see Chapter 4 on buying at an auction).

Whatever your requirements, make sure that the estate agent is aware of them and that you are put on his mailing list to receive details of relevant properties. You will soon get used to estate agents' euphemisms, such as 'ideal for the DIY expert' which usually means that the building is in an extreme state of disrepair. If you are prepared to renovate extensively you may pick up a very good bargain.

Give the estate agent an idea of your price range, the amount you can borrow and how much you intend to set aside for renovation work. If you are sent details of a property above your planned limit you may like to put in an offer for it. Apart from trying to get you to part with more money, the estate agent may be indicating to you that an offer is likely to be accepted. If you see something outside your price limit that you have set your heart on, it may be worth discussing this with your local building society who may be able to help you to find a solution.

The press

Local newspapers are a good source of information and you may be able to spot a bargain this way. By regularly reviewing the property section you will gain an understanding of the local housing market — how prices are increasing or decreasing and the turnover time for different properties in the area.

It is always a good idea to read the regional and national press together with specialist magazines such as *Exchange and Mart*, *Dalton's Weekly* and the *London and Weekly Advertiser*. Those people looking for something grand are advised to consult *Country Life*, *Tatler* and *Harpers and Queen*.

Placing an advertisement in the 'Property Wanted' page of your local newspaper can be beneficial. This may enable you to negotiate a lower price as the vendor will not be paying an agent's commission.

Friends and colleagues

It is worthwhile asking friends and colleagues about areas you are interested in. Not only will you benefit from their personal knowledge and experience but they may also be able to tell you about a property before it comes on the market.

'For sale' boards

Driving around an area will show you which properties are for sale and will give you an indication of which estate agents are active in the area.

What to look out for

Leasehold or freehold

Leasehold property ultimately returns to the ownership of the lessor, ie the freeholder, when the lease expires. Leases are usually granted for periods of 99 or 999 years. If you buy a property with a short lease then it will be harder to sell it for a good price. The Leasehold Reform Act 1967, with some exceptions, gives owners of leasehold houses the right to buy the freehold or extend the lease.

If you intend to restore a leasehold property, bear in mind that improvements need the consent of the freeholder. Repair and maintenance work, on the other hand, do not. In Scotland, where the term 'freehold' has no meaning, the owner of the property should consult the title deeds to ensure that the proposed work does not contravene them.

Freehold property is held in absolute ownership. It is the most common form of tenure for houses in England and Wales. The Scottish equivalent of freehold is feu hold.

Planning permission

Building work is regulated by a variety of statutory controls. If you are buying a property to renovate you must be informed about whether or not planning permission is needed. You will often have to make an application weeks or months in advance of the work starting. It may be that if only certain changes are permitted then you will have to rethink your plans.

If the work you are intending to carry out will result in substantial changes to the external appearance of the property, planning permission should be sought by writing to your local planning authority.

Some works do not require planning permission. These are known as 'permitted development' and include:

- Increases in the volume of the property up to 70 cubic metres or 15 per cent of the original volume
- Conservatories and porches providing that the porch is less than 2

square metres in area, less than 3 metres in height and no closer than 2 metres to the front boundary

- Loft conversions as long as the conversion does not increase the volume of the house or involve the construction of a dormer
- Garden sheds or greenhouses with a maximum height of 3 metres and not bigger than half the size of your garden
- Fences, gates and walls to the front providing they are below 1 metre high; to the rear you can build up to a height of 2 metres.

There are various booklets available giving advice on what does or does not need planning permission. Planning Aid for Londoners has published a *Householder's Guide to Planning Permission* (£1 from the London branch of the Royal Town Planning Institute). The Department of the Environment and the Welsh Office publish a free booklet *Planning Permission: A Guide for Householders*. It is also helpful to visit the planning department of your local authority to discuss your ideas with a planning officer, who can tell you what is likely to be accepted.

If planning permission is required there are certain procedures to follow. You will have to:

- Complete the appropriate forms
- Submit your plans
- Pay the required fee to the local authority (the current fee for an application is £33 for enlargement, improvements or alterations to an existing building).

If your restoration scheme is complicated then you will have to hire a professional to produce the plans (see Chapter 5 on hiring professionals).

The procedure in Scotland is similar. A permitted development for which planning permission is not needed is:

- Extending a house (other than a terraced house) up to 20 per cent of the original size to a maximum of 115 cubic metres.

Planning permission *is* needed for:

- An extension over 4 metres high and within 2 metres of the boundary, or which would occupy over 50 per cent of the curtilage (the area attached to the dwelling).

A notice of application for planning permission must be served on neighbours which tells them where they can inspect the plans and drawings. The current fee for alterations to existing buildings is £27.

Work on the inside of a property does not normally need planning permission; neither do a range of smaller external developments. Exceptions include listed buildings or buildings in specially designated areas such as National Parks.

Listed buildings

Any building that has been listed under the town and country planning legislation, by the Department of the Environment, cannot be demolished, extended or altered in any way that affects its character, inside and outside, without a 'listed building consent' form having been obtained from the local authority. This is an additional requirement to planning permission. The listed buildings are graded and what you can do to them depends on which grade your property is classed within.

If the property you are looking at is listed as being of architectural or historical interest, or is in a conservation area, you should consult the planning department straight away. The advice of a professional is strongly recommended as these buildings are subject to complex legislation. The Royal Town Planning Institute issues a leaflet called *What is Listed Building Consent?* which explains the complexities associated with buying and renovating such properties.

Similar rules apply to listed buildings in Scotland. Details of these buildings are available from the planning department of the local authority. In England, Scotland and Wales, if you carry out work without proper consent the planning authority may serve you with an enforcement notice requiring that you return the listed building to the condition it was in before you started work on it.

If your house is in a conservation area then you will need to seek conservation area consent before starting any work. You should also check to make sure that none of the trees in your garden are subject to tree preservation orders. If you live in a conservation area you will need permission to cut down a tree.

Building regulations

The Building Regulations 1985 stipulate how buildings should be constructed; buildings must conform to these regulations, which are administered by the Building Control Department of your local authority. It is to them that you must apply for building regulations approval. A pamphlet published by the Department of the Environment, *The Manual to the Building Regulations* 1985 (HMSO, £6.20) provides useful guidance on how to interpret the regulations.

Building regulations are there to ensure that a property is structurally sound. Approval must be obtained for most development work to the property both internal and external. However, there are exceptions and you are advised to contact your local authority before commencing work.

There are two methods of obtaining building regulations approval:

- Full plans — this involves submitting a full set of plans to the local authority before the work begins. If these are accepted formal approval will be given.
- Building notice — notice is given in writing to the local authority advising them that you intend to carry out the work. No approval is formally given but the work is inspected 'on site'. The danger is that the building control officer could ask you to do more than you had originally planned.

It is advisable to apply for building regulations approval as soon as possible as it can take several weeks for your application to be processed. Whichever approval method you choose, you will be required to pay a fee and this will vary with the cost of your restoration works.

It is up to you, or the professional acting on your behalf (but you are still responsible for instructing him), to seek building regulations approval. Building control officers are there to advise you and to discuss your plans. Building regulations approval should be sought before you approach builders for quotations. Once your plans are approved, the authority will send you an official form that sets out any further conditions or requirements. They should also send you Building Legislation Inspection Cards which you will need to send to the local authority building control department at appropriate stages in your programme. An officer will then be sent to inspect the work.

The procedure in Scotland varies slightly. Before starting work you must ensure that a building warrant is obtained from the local building control authority. You will then be advised on what details you will need to provide to enable them to check for compliance with the regulations. A fee is payable which varies according to the likely cost of the project. If you are going to carry out demolition work then you will also need to obtain a warrant.

The local authority must be notified when building work begins and then at specified stages. The work may be inspected. You will need to obtain a completions certificate before the new part of the building can be occupied. A building warrant applies only to approval of the standard of construction and, as in England and Wales, you will also need to seek planning permission.

Points to bear in mind when considering potential purchases

As this chapter shows, there are a number of points to remember when considering which property to buy. The following checklist will draw your attention to the most important considerations as highlighted in this chapter.

Checklist

- Pay particular attention to your requirements. Draw up your own list of basic needs and refer to this each time you look at a property.

- Carefully assess what type of property to buy in the light of your basic requirements and also:
  — your budget
  — the type of property you prefer
  — the scale of work you are prepared to undertake
  — the area in which you would like to live.

- Consult as wide a variety of information sources as possible when looking for a property.

- Pay special attention to the requirement of planning permission BEFORE you buy as there is no point in buying a property to restore only to find that the work you envisaged is not permitted.

- The work you commission on your house is subject to building regulations. Make sure that approval is sought BEFORE work begins.

- Listed buildings, or buildings in conservation areas or National Parks, are subject to different rules so familiarise yourself with these if you intend to buy such a property.

You are now ready to secure the home of your choice.

4
Buying a Property

This chapter details the sequence of events that you will follow in purchasing the house of your choice. The first step is to give serious thought to your restoration programme. If the work is going to be extensive including the construction of extra buildings, it is useful to get an architect or surveyor to draw up the plans for you. You should also obtain quotations from builders and contractors, electricians, plumbers etc to give you an idea of what the work is likely to cost. Your plans and quotations will enable you to assess the scale of the programme and how long the work is going to take. Chapters 5 and 6 offer advice on using professionals to run the works programme for you and on organising this yourself.

Once you have discussed your ideas with your building society you may decide to make an offer on the property subject to contract and survey.

Making an offer

The fact that you have made an offer on a property establishes your formal interest in it. The offer is made to the vendor or his agent. Before making the offer it is advisable to establish whether there are any other offers on the property and, if so, how many. If there are a number of offers you should think carefully before proceeding. It may be that your offer will be used solely as a means to push up the asking price.

Any offer must be made subject to contract and survey. This ensures that you do not have to pay the vendor's costs if you decide to withdraw. Do not put in an offer unless you are serious about going ahead.

When deciding how much to offer it is useful to consider:

- How long the property has been on the market
- How many other people have made an offer.

Your decision will reflect:

- How keen you are to secure the property
- What you can afford to pay.

You should be guided by your knowledge of the local area which may give you an indication of how much the property is worth. If you have looked at a number of properties in the area and scanned the local press regularly then you may get a good idea of whether or not the asking price is reasonable.

The speed with which you act will depend on:

- Which part of the country you live in
- Whether it is a buyer's or a seller's market.

If you are buying in a seller's market you will have to persuade the vendor that you are the best person to sell to. You could use the following arguments:

- As a first-time buyer you will not have a property to sell and can therefore proceed at the vendor's pace
- If you are not a first-time buyer but have sold your house the same will apply (unless of course anything goes wrong higher up the chain)
- Producing a certificate from the building society saying that they have set aside money to lend you will help to sway the vendor in your favour.

Once the offer has been made you may be asked to pay a holding deposit both as a gesture of goodwill and to show that you are serious about buying the property. The deposit should only be given subject to contract and survey and you should obtain a receipt stating this. If the transaction is abandoned, for example after an unsatisfactory survey, the deposit must be returned. At this stage, the estate agent will take the name and address of your solicitor or conveyancer.

Valuations and surveys

If your offer is accepted and you wish to arrange a mortgage then the building society will be required to carry out a valuation of the property. The type of valuation will depend on the sort of mortgage that you require. If a traditional mortgage is used to buy the property then a standard valuation is all that is needed. The valuation is required to ensure that the property is worth at least the amount you intend to borrow. If you have opted for the National and Provincial's House Restoration Mortgage then a more complex valuation will be necessary. This is because the building society is interested not only in the current value of the building but also in its likely future value after your restoration work is completed. In carrying out a valuation, the building society valuer may also request that special reports are carried out.

It is important to note that a building society valuation is for mortgage purposes only and does not guarantee that a property is structurally sound or that it is worth the asking price. The cost of a valuation will depend on the asking price of the house. The more expensive the property, and the more complex the valuation, the more you will pay. Building societies have leaflets setting out how much you will have to pay for valuation, and properties are divided into price brackets.

Valuation takes into account the following characteristics of a property:

- Age, type, accommodation, fixtures and features
- Construction and general state of repair
- Siting and general local amenities
- Tenure, tenancies, annual payments and liabilities.

The more complex valuation undertaken for the National and Provincial's House Restoration Mortgage differs in that it also takes your restoration plans into account and can provide a value for the property in its renovated condition. This enables you to carry out repairs and improvements as part of your mortgage.

Before progressing with the purchase it is likely that your building society will recommend that you have a full structural survey carried out. In some instances you may be able to save money by arranging with the building society for the valuation and full structural survey to be carried out at the same time.

Once the valuation, structural survey and any other specialist reports have been carried out, the building society will advise you on precisely how much they are able to lend you to purchase this particular property. If you have chosen a house restoration mortgage then the amount of money that will be released to you as each job is completed will also be agreed.

If you decide to have a full structural survey carried out, the building society may be able to provide you with a list of local surveyors. Alternatively, information on surveyors who undertake structural surveys can be obtained from the Royal Institution of Chartered Surveyors (RICS). Like other professionals, the surveyor is liable to you, the client, if he makes a negligent omission and, when discussing your needs with him, you should ask for confirmation that he holds professional indemnity insurance cover.

The survey can only be as thorough as the property allows. It can cover only what is visible and it is unlikely that the vendor will let your surveyor take up carpets to look at the state of the floorboards. If you are buying a ground floor flat it is unlikely that your surveyor will be given access to the roof void through the top flat. Despite this, the surveyor is trained to spot signs of serious problems and it is possible to agree the extent of the survey beforehand and any specialist testing that needs to take place.

In his report to you the surveyor will highlight major and minor problems and it is up to you to decide how seriously each of these will affect your decision to go ahead with the purchase. Every property will have some faults. If the survey reveals that a great deal of major work is needed urgently you could use this to negotiate a lower price for the house. If you are renovating a property you may purposely have chosen somewhere that needs major structural work and have only to make sure that the asking price reflects this.

The legal process

Keep in close contact with your solicitor throughout the buying process so that you can both react quickly if things start to go in an unanticipated direction. Some vendors are unscrupulous and let more than one buyer start to purchase the property — unfortunately, costs will often have been incurred before the buyer finds that he is not alone. Another pitfall of the system in England and Wales is 'gazumping'. This is when the vendor accepts a higher offer than yours for his house, and may use this to get you to offer more. You then have to weigh up how much money you have lost already and whether or not to back out. There will often be no choice as you cannot borrow any more money. If your mortgage is arranged through the National and Provincial Building Society, for example, you will be able to arrange free anti-gazumping cover, if you are a first-time buyer, through their Homepack Insurance option.

The term 'conveyancing' refers to the process of conveying the ownership of the property from one party to another. In England and Wales you have the choice of:

- Appointing your own solicitor
- Choosing a licensed conveyancer
- Doing the conveyancing yourself.

If you have a mortgage, the building society may insist that a solicitor is employed for some of the work.

The best way to find a solicitor is to have one recommended to you by your building society or friends. It is noteworthy that you may save costs if you choose to use the same solicitor as the building society. Lists of licensed conveyancers can be obtained from the Council of Licensed Conveyancers or the Association of Licensed Conveyancers. It is prudent to get a detailed quote before deciding who to use, as rates vary considerably.

Your solicitor will perform many tasks as part of the conveyancing process. The main elements include:

- Checking that the property is as described, is for sale by the vendor, and has no technical difficulties associated with it
- Checking that there are no compulsory purchase orders on it

- Ensuring that a demolition order does not threaten the property or that extensive repairs are not imposed by the Environmental Health Department
- Checking the deeds of the property
- Drawing up a contract for sale
- Explaining to you the terms freehold and leasehold
- Exchanging contracts.

You are unlikely to be able to sign and exchange contracts until all the checking is completed. Your solicitor will have sent off for local authority searches to be carried out. Once the results of these have come back, together with the outcome of his preliminary enquiries and confirmation of ownership, and agreement has been made for a completion date, you can think about exchanging contracts.

Contracts

You and the vendor each have identical copies of the contract drawn up by your respective solicitors. These are then exchanged and signed by the other party. As from exchange, the contract is legally binding and the transaction must take place. At this stage, approximately 10 per cent of the purchase price of the house is handed over. There is then a period of about four weeks before completion occurs. This is when the rest of the money is transferred to the vendor and the property becomes yours. If the property costs over £30,000 then stamp duty is payable on the whole price at a rate of 1 per cent. Make sure that your solicitor has made arrangements for the balance of the payment to be made. The vendor's solicitor gives your solicitor the legal document which transfers to you the title to the land.

Buying in Scotland

Buying in Scotland has many similarities but also some differences from buying in the rest of the UK. As well as the press, the main sources of information about property in Scotland are solicitors and estate agents. Solicitors sell the most property in Scotland and many have established property centres. A list of these can be obtained from the Law Society of Scotland. Some solicitors have their own property departments. Estate agents are gaining a hold on the Scottish market and operate as in the rest of the UK.

Almost all property is bought and sold with the help of a solicitor. If the property is over £30,000 then stamp duty of 1 per cent of this sum is paid. There will also be registration charges for the Register of Sasines or Land Register in Scotland.

Surveys on the property take place before an offer is made. This means that you could lose the property to a higher bidder after having gone to the expense of commissioning a survey. Once the offer has been accepted, a binding agreement is made. The two solicitors will then exchange 'missives', the legally binding contracts. The title deeds and disposition are exchanged for the payment of a cheque and this completes the purchase. This can happen as quickly as a few days after the exchange of missives.

Buying at an auction

Auctions are usually conducted by estate agents and can be a useful source of property, especially if you are looking for something out of the ordinary such as a barn or farmhouse. Take care not to get carried away by the atmosphere at an auction which can tempt you to offer far too much. Much of the property on offer will require considerable renovation and, until very recently, it has been difficult to secure a building society mortgage on such property. It is sensible to get the backing of the building society, at least in principle, before putting in your offer.

Mistakes can be avoided by preparing before the auction. The auction programme is available from the estate agent or auctioneer a few weeks before the event. If you obtain this early enough you can quiz the agent about the properties that interest you.

When bidding, it is useful to have worked out your maximum offer. In order to do this, you should estimate how much the restoration work will cost. Some properties will be more expensive but require less work, so decide what type of property to bid for. If your bid is accepted, the contract of sale is drawn up on the back of the auction catalogue and you will be required to sign then and there. This is equivalent to exchanging contracts. You will almost certainly be expected to hand over approximately 10 per cent of the purchase money in cash. The balance is paid within an agreed period from the auction date — usually two weeks. If the balance is not paid then, you could forfeit your claim. If, however, the vendor feels that the delay was unavoidable he may extend the 'completion date'.

Some auctions are organised on the basis of 'sealed bids'. This means that each bidder writes down his offer and this is sealed in an envelope. The highest bid is accepted. Bidders are guided by a minimum offer. The obvious disadvantage from your point of view is that you have no idea what anyone else is bidding and do not have a chance to raise the offer. This form of auction is used for properties that have failed to reach their reserve price at an open auction.

Summary of tips to remember when buying a property

1. *The offer* — you do not have to offer the asking price. Check how many offers there are already for that property. Find out how long it has been on the market. Make your offer subject to contract, a satisfactory survey, and searches.
2. *The deposit* — Always ask for a receipt which states that the deposit is returnable and subject to contract, survey and searches.
3. *The valuation and survey* — ascertain what sort of valuation will take place. This will depend on the type of mortgage you have opted for. If you are going to carry out extensive restoration work then a full structural survey is also recommended. Commissioning the valuation and survey to be done at the same time by the same surveyor will reduce your costs.
4. *The legal process* — Spend time deciding whether to appoint a solicitor or conveyancer or to do the conveyancing yourself. Speak to your solicitor on a regular basis to ease communication and lessen the likelihood of the purchase running into serious difficulties.
5. *Contracts* — Remember to instruct your solicitor to have the balance of the money available for completion.
6. *Auctions* — It will pay you to work out how much a property is worth and then add to this how much you will have to spend on restoring it. This is then your true cost and will influence how much you can afford to bid.

Remaining calm and unemotional through the buying process is a considerable feat. It will be to your advantage if you can do this as you will then be less likely to make mistakes. Once you have crossed the hurdle of buying the property you can begin the fun — restoring it.

PART 2

THE RESTORATION PROCESS

5

If You Choose to Use a Professional

Deciding whether to oversee the restoration process yourself or whether to leave this to someone else is one of the most important decisions you will have to make and therefore requires careful thought. If you are renovating the property in which you already live then it will be easier to oversee the work should you want to. If you are restoring another property, which could be some distance from where you live, then you have to consider the extra cost of having to visit the site regularly. You may decide in this case to hand over control to someone else. If you choose to manage the work yourself then you will need somewhere nearby where you can stay.

Factors affecting your decision to retain day-to-day control of the restoration work or to surrender this to a professional will include:

- The scale of the work and its likely cost
- Your competence to oversee the work: Will it be too technically complicated? Have you done this before?
- The amount of time you have to spare: Can you take time off work? What will be the cost to you? Do you want to spend all your spare time on the project?

- How much the work will cost: Does your building society or bank insist on your seeking professional advice?
- Will there be any future maintenance work? If so, do you want to commit yourself to overseeing this too?

You will get the best results from your restoration programme if you are clear about what you want and can communicate your wishes to others. This applies whether you hire a professional to take charge or do this yourself. However small or large the scale of your restoration programme you will save time and money by setting aside a few hours at the onset to decide what you want. Looking through some of the many DIY books on the market not only will suggest ideas to you but also will give you an indication of how these can be put into practice. If you know you want to extend the kitchen, for example, but can only think of one way of doing this, scanning books will give you alternatives. You should also consider what level of quality you will be looking for in the finished job. Do you want the extension to look basic and practical or to be individualistic and high-class? Your budget will control this to some extent, but by consulting books and professionals you will get a better idea of what you can achieve within your budget and the alternatives available. Remember that it will be difficult to instruct others (a) if you do not have a clear idea of what you want yourself and (b) if you keep changing your mind. This chapter is for those people who decide to hand over responsibility for their restoration programme to a professional.

Types of professional and their roles

The two types of professional that you are most likely to choose for planning and carrying out the work are architects and surveyors. Generally speaking, if you require a high level of design expertise then an architect is commonly used. If most of the work involves changes to existing buildings, such as extensions or internal alterations, then a surveyor will be your obvious choice.

Architects

Only suitably qualified persons registered with the Architects' Registration Council are permitted to call themselves architects. The professional institution for architects is the Royal Institute of British Architects (RIBA) but not all architects belong to RIBA. RIBA's equivalent in Scotland is the Royal Incorporation of Architects in Scotland, and ARIAS or FRIAS indicate membership or fellowship of this body. Architects can be used for landscape design or interior design where creativity is needed.

Surveyors (chartered)

Only members of the Royal Institution of Chartered Surveyors (RICS) can use the term 'chartered surveyor'. The type of surveyor you will need will depend on the nature of the work. RICS is divided into several divisions, of which General Practice and Building Surveyors are two. You are most likely to need the latter who are trained to deal with new construction work and repairs, alterations, extensions and adaptations to existing buildings. RICS can provide you with the name of someone in your local area.

Other professionals

Other professional bodies include the Incorporated Association of Architects and Surveyors (IAAS) and the Faculty of Architects and Surveyors (FAS). Although they do not have the status or training of the architect or chartered surveyor, many other professionals and technicians carry out design and drawing work. Technicians may belong to the Society of Surveying Technicians (designatory letters: MSST), or the British Institute of Architectural Technicians (designatory letters: MBIAT) among other technical bodies within the construction industry. Traditionally, technicians have been associated with putting other people's ideas into practice but some have set up on their own and are self-employed. If you find a suitably qualified technician he may be able to carry out your requirements at reasonable cost.

How much do professionals charge?

RIBA and RICS provide guidelines for fees that you can expect their members to charge. These are only guidelines and you cannot hold people to them, but they will give you some idea of the sorts of costs to budget for which are usually worked out as a percentage of the total construction work. Not all professionals will charge for their time in this way; some will opt for an hourly rate. If this is the case remember to insist that proper records are kept. You may want to put a ceiling on the amount you will pay if you are being charged an hourly rate.

If you are employing a professional for a conventional percentage fee to plan and oversee a building project then you are buying his 'basic services'. RIBA's *Architectural Appointment* (£2 from RIBA Publications, Kingsbury Mission, Moreland Street, London EC1V 8BB) outlines what an architect's services are, the conditions which normally apply, recommended fees and expenses, and an example of an agreement and a schedule.

RIBA's payment system is worked out according to a series of work stages as described below.

Work stages A and B relate to discussion, inspection of the property, suggestions and advice on feasibility.

Work Stage C — Outline proposals: your requirements are discussed, together with estimates of cost.

Work stage D — Scheme design: the design is set out so that decisions on style, materials and appearance are covered. A more accurate estimate of costs is produced. Dates are put forward for starting and completing the work. Application for planning permission is sent off if needed.

Work stage E — Detailed design: construction costs, quality of materials and standard of workmanship are discussed here. Quotes are obtained for specialist work. Applications for building regulations approval and other statutory requirements are made now.

Work stages F and G — Production information: final drawings are produced and the specifications put together in significant detail to go out to contractors for quotes.

Work stage H — Tendering: advice is given as to which contractors should 'tender' for a job. You will be advised on which tender to accept.

Work stage J — Project planning: this covers the contract which you and the contractor will sign.

Work stage K — Operations on site: work starts and professional checks are made to ensure that it is being carried out in accordance with the specifications and drawings.

Work Stage L — Completion: you should be advised as to whether the work has been satisfactorily completed and whether regular maintenance is needed.

Payment is made on the basis of a percentage of total construction work. RIBA's recommended percentages are set out in Table 5.1.

Work stage	**Proportion of fee** %	**Cumulative total** %
C	15	15
D	20	35
E	20	55
F,G	20	75
H,J,K,L	25	100

Table 5.1 Percentage payment to professionals

Jobs additional to these basic services are charged over and above the percentage fee and are usually calculated on an hourly rate. Do seek competitive quotes as these can vary considerably. The going rate at present is about £15–25 per hour for an architect or surveyor, £9–12 per hour for a technician. Extra fees could be incurred through long meetings with the planning department, for example. You must agree at the onset:

- what will be classified as extra services
- what rate you will pay and up to what limit
- that the professional keeps clear records of the time spent on work other than that outlined in the work stages.

If you choose to combine the work of a professional with your own skills then you will pay for partial services. You could use a professional to help you to plan the work, for example, but oversee it yourself. His work will then be charged at an hourly rate. Using a professional adviser to help you choose an architect or surveyor is also an option. Although this involves yet more money, the time saved on getting quotes could allow the work to begin earlier. The professional adviser is also likely to get you the best rates and will save you the money you will be paying him in fees.

The professional you have hired to oversee the work may, at times, need to seek additional specialist help. For example, loading calculations may be needed for a structural engineer if you intend to knock large holes through walls. These extra costs will also be your responsibility so remember to allow for them. The expenses incurred by everyone working on the site have also to be met. Travel costs, hotel bills, telephone bills, postage costs etc must all be budgeted for. It is advisable to get a rough estimate of these expenses at the outset.

If your professional is VAT registered then 15 per cent will automatically be added to the bill. This is easy to forget! Looking for someone who is not VAT registered is not a way out, as it might mean that that person is new to the business or is working part-time. You could well be making a false economy by trying to avoid paying VAT. Payment is made at the end of each work stage and should be made promptly.

What can you reasonably expect the professional to do on your behalf?

Having been thoroughly briefed by you, the professional will survey the site. If you are beginning work on the house you live in it is useful to have a full structural survey carried out, especially if the house has not been surveyed for years. This will show up any defects which can be put right while the other work is going on. It will also serve as a valuable reference document. If extra damage is caused to your property then it will be easier to prove this. If you do not have the original plans of the house the professional will have to draw up new ones. It is at the survey stage that any hazardous substances in the property, for example asbestos, will show up and can be dealt with.

Your input into the design process is crucial. You cannot leave someone to come up with a design for a bedroom only to tell them afterwards that the antique Edwardian wardrobe does not fit in. If the design has to be redone because you failed to brief the architect fully then you will have to pay for your mistake.

An agreement is now drawn up between the professional and the owner of the building (his client, ie *you*). Your professional will seek quotations from builders and will negotiate the builders' conditions of work. Your agreement with the professional will include such things as:

- work to be carried out
- services that the professional will supply
- control of the works — to include issues such as site visits, meetings with contractors, reporting back to you, payment conditions.

It is beyond the scope of this book to go into contracts in great detail; if you want to go into this further, you are advised to consult some of the publications listed at the end of this book.

While the work is in progress the professional is your representative and acts as a go-between for you and the builders. He must inspect the work from time to time and report back to you on its progress. If you have any worries or complaints these should be channelled through your architect or surveyor. Meetings on site should take place every couple of weeks between you, the professional and the contractors.

Costs are bound to rise, especially if you are having major work done over a long period of time. However well the plans have been prepared, there are always unforeseeable problems. Where the professional has to make sure that extra work is done he should confirm this in writing to you.

Subcontracting

Some specialised work may be put out to a subcontractor. Neither you nor the professional will be able to influence the choice of subcontractor. What you can do though is to have nominated a subcontractor in advance and to have had this built into your agreement with the professional. Subcontractors will require special facilities such as scaffolding, rubbish removal etc; these should all be provided — otherwise you run the risk of the subcontractor turning up, finding that you do not have what he needs, and charging you for a wasted trip.

Summary of points for employing a professional to run the site for you

1. Communicate regularly with your architect or surveyor but do not interfere unnecessarily with what he is doing. On no account must you go straight to the builders if you think something is wrong.
2. Try to establish good working relations with everyone whether or not you are living on site.
3. Have regular meetings with the professional to find out how the work is progressing.
4. Ensure that full records are kept by the professional and that you are advised in writing immediately he knows of extra costs.

6
If You Choose to Run the Site Yourself

In this chapter it is assumed that you have chosen to run the site yourself and not to hand over entirely to a professional although you might use a professional for specific jobs. Your best weapon in the face of such a challenge is thorough planning. This applies both to the initial conceptual stage and also to the day-to-day coordination of activities on site. As in Chapter 5, the advice in this chapter is for people who are doing up their own home and live on site and for others who are directing operations from a distance. It covers major and minor projects — from rebuilding the inside of a house to repairing the guttering.

Planning the programme

Your first step is to decide what you want done and to what quality you want the work finished. Consulting a comprehensive DIY book will not only give you ideas but will also show you what is possible. You could also contact the Building Research Establishment (BRE), which provides information on the construction industry and offers a range of publications. Their address is given at the end of this book.

Once you have decided what you want you can begin to produce a breakdown of the work and a schedule telling you roughly how long each phase will take. By combining the two, you can produce a programme for use on site so that you can see at a glance how fast the work is progressing. This will help you to plan for the arrival of contractors.

Your task will be made that much easier if the work is arranged so that one job leads on from another. For example, once new drainage and a new manhole are laid, the complete installation and testing of internal plumbing can take place. Time devoted at the planning stage to the sequence of operations is critical and can save a lot of time and money.

As well as your work programme, it is advisable to keep a site diary. Events should be recorded daily. Six months later you may need to look up when a contractor visited the site and how long he spent there — these are not the sort of details that you will be able to recall if you do not keep proper records.

Figure 6.1 shows an example of a typical programme for a small site. The vertical column gives the various items of work — you could also add the contractor's name here. The horizontal column shows the number of weeks that you can expect each item of work to take based on the contractor's estimate. Make sure that you do not book the work so that everyone arrives at once. Certain jobs will have to overlap, however, or the work will never be finished.

Table 6.1 shows a typical estimate and schedule of renovation including labour and materials. Costs will vary depending on the scale of the work you are undertaking but this will give you an indication of the sort of list you should prepare when doing your initial planning and costing. This list, accompanied by estimates and quotes where appropriate, should be used to take to the building society to show how your costs are spread and is the basis for your works programme.

An alternative works programme is shown in Figure 6.2, this time for a kitchen extension. The same principles apply, and the programme details which jobs need to be carried out first. There is no point in arranging for the roof to be erected until all the walls are finished and new plaster may be damaged by the weather if any roof leaks have not been sealed beforehand.

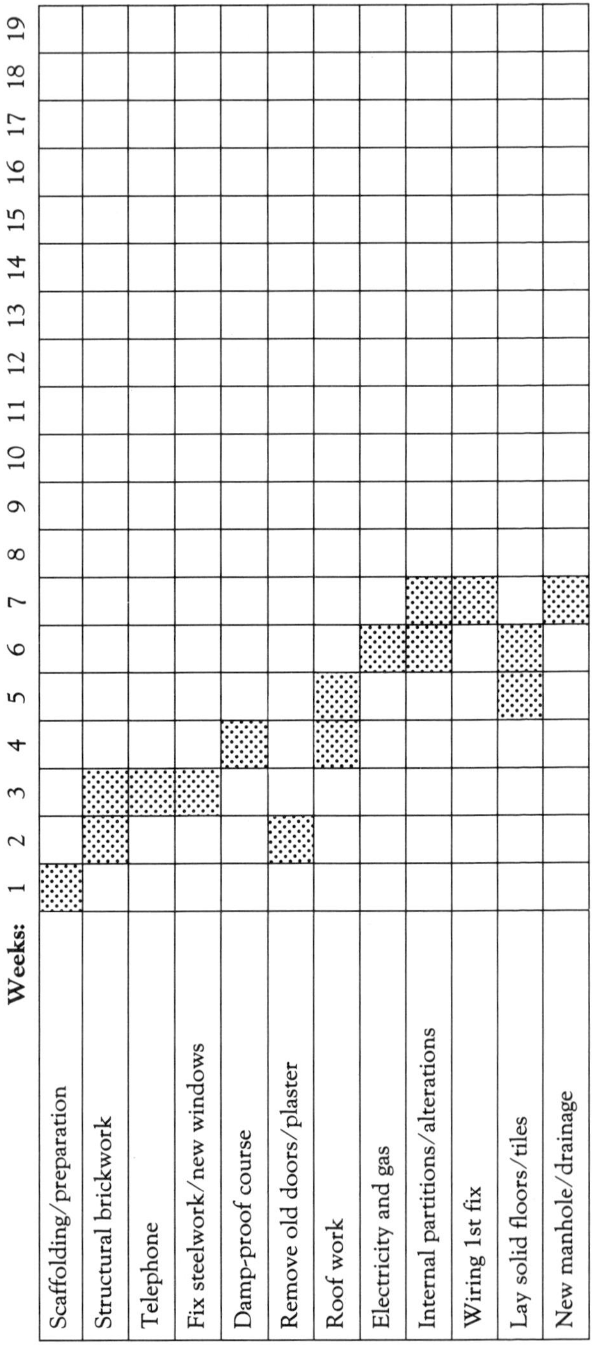
Weeks: 1 2 3 4 5 6 7 8 9 10 11 12 13 14 15 16 17 18 19
Scaffolding/preparation
Structural brickwork
Telephone
Fix steelwork/new windows
Damp-proof course
Remove old doors/plaster
Roof work
Electricity and gas
Internal partitions/alterations
Wiring 1st fix
Lay solid floors/tiles
New manhole/drainage

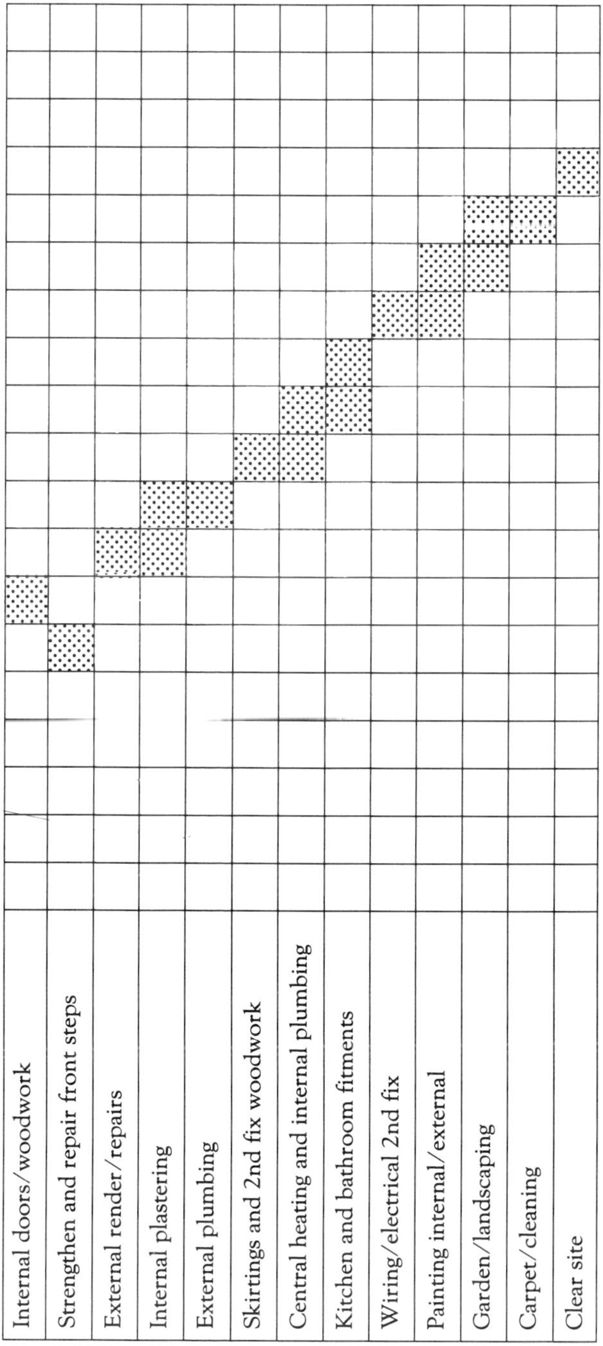

Figure 6.1 A typical programme for a small site

Table 6.1 A typical estimate and schedule of renovation including labour and materials

Item	Cost £	Time
Scaffolding/preparation	1,200	1 week
Structural brickwork	900	1½ weeks
Site telephone (including calls)	300	—
Supporting beams (steel work)	350	3 days
New windows	1,450	3 days
Damp-proof course/timber treatment	1,400	4 days
Remove old plaster work/timber	180	2 days
New roof and guttering	1,900	2 weeks
New electricity and gas supplies	550	3 days
Internal partition work	900	2 weeks
Electrical installation	1,800	2 weeks
Basement solid floor and tiles	1,100	2 weeks
New manhole/drainage	650	1 week
Internal doors/woodwork	1,800	2 weeks
Strengthen/repair front steps and cellar	350	3 days
External sand/cement render and repairs	900	1 week
Internal plastering	2,200	2 weeks
Plumbing — internal/external	900	1½ weeks
Central heating/hot water	2,000	1½ weeks
Kitchen and bathroom fixtures	1,900	2 weeks
Painting/decoration — internal/external	1,900	2 weeks
Garden/landscaping	600	1½ weeks
Carpets	900	3 days
Skips/rubbish clearance	350	—
Cleaning/clearing site	200	2 days
Contingencies	1,200	—
Fees (solicitors/estate agents/etc)	2,500	—

It is very important to draw up your own works programme before you go on to commission the work.

Using others

The help of a professional will be needed if you require drawings, for example, so that planning permission and/or building regulations can be complied with. If you do not want to draw up your own schedule

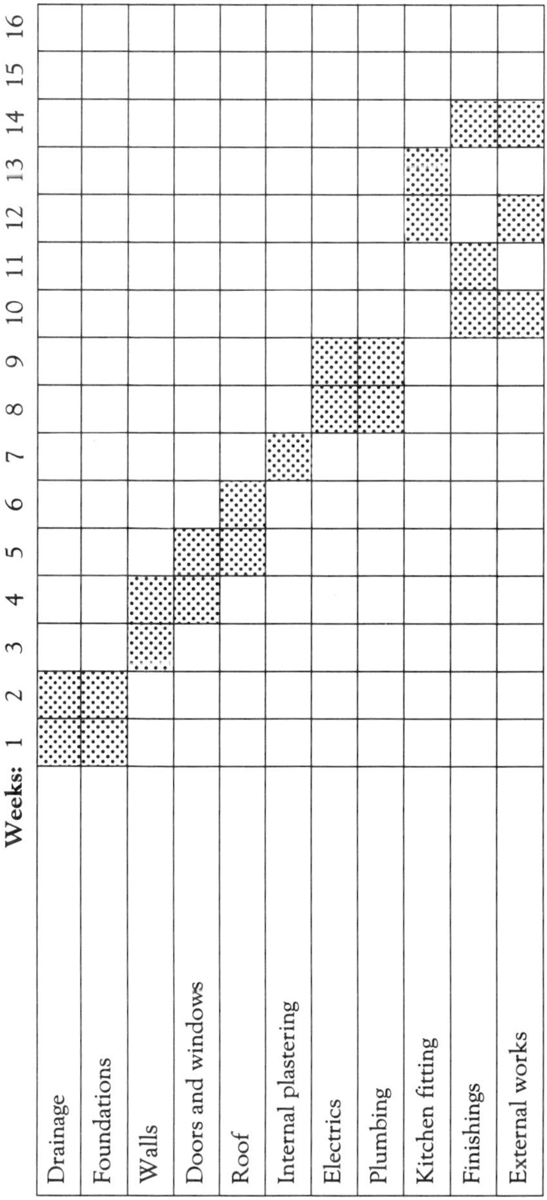

Figure 6.2 A works programme for a kitchen extension

then you could get a chartered building surveyor to do this on your behalf. He could provide you with costings and recommend builders in your area whom he knows to be thorough. You could then take over and supervise the work yourself. The use of professionals as outlined above will be on the basis of 'partial services' and you will be charged at an hourly rate. You may decide not to hire a professional but to let the builder carry out the designs for you, as many builders now offer design expertise.

For the work itself, you will need one or a number of builders. As with architects and surveyors, there are certain qualifications to look for when choosing who to employ. A builder with the designation MCIOB after his name is a member of the Chartered Institute of Building (CIOB). If you choose a chartered builder then you will have some recourse if things go wrong. Other organisations that denote a certain status are the Building Employers Confederation (BEC) and the Federation of Master Builders (FMB). (Chapter 9 covers the codes of practice for these organisations.) Your choice should also reflect whether or not the builder is registered with the National House Builders' Council (NHBC).

When you come to choose a builder, there are a number of questions that you can ask him over the telephone. If the builder is reluctant to answer the questions then find someone else. You could check:

- How long the firm has been established.
- If it is OK if you take up references attesting to the firm's experience of this type of work.
- Whether you can obtain an inter-bank reference through your bank to be assured of their financial stability? (You should then be given the name and address of the firm's bank.)
- If the firm employs all of its own labour or if it subcontracts. (If work is subcontracted, to whom is it put out and how long has the firm known them?)
- If the firm will take responsibility for work that is subcontracted and for all the payments made.
- How the firm wants to be paid and whether you will be invoiced for the work.
- Whether the firm carries third party and employer's liability and if you can see a valid insurance certificate before work begins.
- That the contractor has extended insurance cover such as a contractors' or risks insurance.

- Whether the contract will be subject to a six-month maintenance period.

Another possibility, if you do not want to put out all the work to a team of builders, would be to use separate contractors for each job. You could divide your programme into:

- Work which can be undertaken by a general builder
- Specialist work for which a firm of contractors must be hired.

If you use a different firm of contractors for each job you could get a very good result, possibly at a lower cost, but you will need to spend more of your time and energy organising and coordinating the work. If you want a builder to coordinate the use of contractors then you will obviously have to pay extra for this service. Whatever option you select will depend on your time, energy and commitment. If you want less hassle then you should let someone else handle this.

Obtaining quotations

To get the best price for work on site you should ask a limited number of builders to provide quotations for their work. Quotes are far preferable to estimates as the latter can vary. Once you have been given a quotation you should not be asked to pay more. Beware of making changes to your requirements after the quotation has been given.

It is not worth asking for numerous quotes because each one will cost the builder money as he will have to visit the site and estimate the workload. The money he spends on this will ultimately be passed on to the consumer, ie *you*. It is therefore only worth asking those builders in whom you are genuinely interested.

If you want builders to tender for the job make sure that you are not approaching someone who is already booked up. As an approximate guide, for work that you expect to cost up to £20,000 go to three builders. If it will be over £20,000 then go to four. Each builder whom you want to tender should be sent the same tendering documents containing:

- contract conditions
- specification and any drawings.

In your covering letter you should ask for how long the quote is valid and whether or not the quote includes VAT. Do not try to play one party off against another by showing them a lower quote. This will get a very bad reception in the building trade. Once you have decided which offer to accept, you can draw up a contract. Because there are so many different types of contract it may be useful to consult 'Agreement for Minor Building Works', which is a useful contract produced by the Joint Contracts Tribunal (JCT). A copy of this can be obtained from RIBA (£3.30 plus VAT, plus 10 per cent postage) or from RICS.

Managing work in progress

The amount of immediate preparation you will need to do before the work starts will depend on whether you will be living in the property while you are renovating it or whether you leave the property unoccupied for the whole or part of the renovation programme. Considerations such as sending the kids off to stay with the grandparents or putting the family dog in kennels will only apply if you are living on site. These are concerns that you will have to anticipate and plan for.

Conditions relating to builders' behaviour on site will have been set out in their contract. If you have any grievances, always go through the builder in charge and try to maintain good relations with him and everyone else on site. Regular meetings with the chief builder will ensure that you are kept up to date with the progress of the work and should help to prevent difficulties. A record of any arrangements you have made should be kept for future reference.

Buying and hiring materials and arranging for deliveries

You have to choose between having materials delivered and collecting them yourself. Many builders' merchants offer free deliveries and this can save you a great deal of time as well as aggravation. If possible, you should look for someone who can deliver on the same day. This has two obvious advantages:

- Same-day deliveries reduce the risk of you or your supplier forgetting to make the necessary arrangements for delivery. This may sound obvious but when you are involved in coordinating so many activities it is easy to forget.
- Companies that deliver on the same day as the order is placed tend to be friendlier, more cooperative *and* more efficient.

Most equipment can be hired. Apart from the basics — electric drills, screwdrivers etc — hiring can be advantageous. It saves you having to store equipment (and find it when you need it) and means that breakdowns are replaced at no cost providing they were not your fault. Hired tools and equipment can also be delivered to the site.

Manning the site

As with all the activities that have been described so far, the key words are:

- planning
- programming
- coordination
- efficiency.

To ensure the smooth running of operations you will need some sort of system for dealing efficiently with correspondence and for storing invoices and all your paperwork so that everything is easily retrievable. If you are often out, and are lucky enough to have an answerphone, urgent business can be followed up immediately.

You should carefully keep receipts, accounts, drawings and other paperwork relating to the daily operation of the site. Records of *all* expenditure should be kept, including:

- payment for materials
- payment for work done by others
- payments to yourself.

Record transactions *as they occur*, not two days later when you have forgotten the details. File all bank statements, planning approvals and letters. Keep copies of all your correspondence and file them immediately. File contractors' invoices, receipts for payment — even books. Answer your letters promptly, especially those from local authority departments, gas and electricity boards and the Inland Revenue.

Controlling costs and payments

Cost control schedules

Cost control schedules are an effective way of keeping track of money. They consist of recording all the jobs with the cost for each one in the left hand margin. Across the top of the sheet you put headings for 'supplier', 'date of payment', 'amount'. You can then tell at a glance exactly when you have to provide money and how much is due. If you want a more detailed cost control schedule you can include columns headed 'estimate cost', 'actual cost', 'amount over/under schedule'. This will tell you exactly how you stand at any one time in relation to the cost of the job.

Paying the builder
As suggested above, terms should have been agreed initially. How and when you pay will depend on the nature of the work. If it is a small job the builder will probably be happy to be paid at the end of it. If the work is going to be spread over a couple of months then the builder may require stage payments to be made. NEVER PAY A BUILDER BEFORE HE STARTS WORK. The only exception to this rule is if you are paying a specialist to carry out a specific task — for example installing double glazing. These firms usually require a deposit before they start work (see Chapter 9 for Codes of Practice relating to double glazing firms).

Where agreed, stage payments should only be made for work as the stages are satisfactorily completed. You will have to pay an additional 15 per cent for VAT if the builder is VAT registered. At the end of this contract when the 'final account' is to be paid, your builder should give you a statement which shows:

- any differentiation in the original contract sum
- the cost of any additions or omissions
- any retentions held back during the defects liability period (see Chapter 9)
- the final adjusted contract sum.

From this total, deduct the sum of any interim payment.

'Extra work' (extras)
There are bound to be unforeseen costs. You should ask the builder to inform you of these in writing immediately. It may be difficult to check that you have been charged correctly for these extras. One tip is to see if the original quote included similar work that can be used as a guide to what these extras should be.

Ask the builder to provide a breakdown of the costs into:

- cost of materials
- costs of labour.

You then have some idea of what the cost of materials should be and can isolate the labour costs. It is helpful to agree a rate for labour costs BEFORE WORK BEGINS. Do not agree to pay extras on an open-ended daily rate as the work could go on for months.

How to pay

The need to keep records of payments with the date they were made cannot be over-emphasised. If you pay by cheque then the cheque book stub must always be filled in. If you pay for anything with cash it may be useful to buy a cash book for entering these payments.

If you have opted for a House Restoration Mortgage, you will need to keep copies of your invoices and send the originals to your building society so that they can reimburse you for work that has been completed.

Safety and Security

- Ask to see your builder's insurance policy and make sure *his* name is on it
- Inform your insurance company when the work will start and keep them informed if the date changes
- Make sure that access to the property is sealed off when it is unattended.

The Health and Safety at Work Act 1974 covers all construction and restoration work. It is the builder's responsibility to comply with this Act and to ensure that his staff are working in safe conditions.

Try to plan so that all the jobs that affect security take place early on, so that if someone breaks in there will be nothing worth taking.

Requirements for effective site management

- Spend adequate time deciding what you want and drawing up a work programme.
- Keep records of everything you do and everything you spend. Efficient management of the work will pay dividends.
- Decide how many other people to use — professionals, builders,

specialist contractors. Choose suitably qualified and, preferably, recommended tradesmen.

- Work out how materials will be paid for, whether to hire equipment, to have them delivered or to collect them yourself.
- Draw up cost control schedules and work out how payments will be made and when they are due. Allow for 'extra work'.
- Pay due care and attention to matters of health and safety.

7
A Typical Renovation Programme

This chapter looks at some of the jobs that will have to be carried out in a typical renovation programme. The chapter should be read bearing in mind the advice given in Chapters 5 and 6. Our aim is to give you an idea of what the work entails.

Before you start the work you must submit formal notice to the Building Inspector/Borough Surveyor/District Surveyor telling him that the project is about to commence. (See Chapter 3 on Building Regulations.) This is done by filling in a standard postcard which is obtained from his office.

Preparing the site

Depending on the state of the house and the nature of the work that you intend to carry out, demolition and clearing may be necessary. The most efficient way to clear the site is to construct a shute leading from the upper floor window to the ground. If there is to be any demolition then order the rubbish skips in advance. The demolition work should start at the top of the building, with rubble being fed down the shute into a bin. When the bin is full the contents are transferred to the skip.

During this stage of the renovation programme the following should be done:

- Old ceilings stripped out
- Old plaster removed if it is to be replaced
- Plaster hacked away to make room for the new damp course
- Old timber, eg rotten doors, floorboards, etc, removed
- Water and gas supplies and old wiring and conduit uncovered and cleared.

The damp proof course (DPC)

A damp proof course prevents rising damp. It consists of a membrane of non-permeable material laid between courses of brick about 15 centimetres above ground level. The damp proof course runs all the way round the house.

There are four ways of laying the damp course:

- The existing brickwork is removed 1 metre at a time at the right height and replaced with a bituminous felt or vinyl DPC between the two courses removed
- A series of connecting copper rods are drilled into the walls. These act as a DPC by electrolytic action
- A series of porcelain caps are installed at the correct height all the way around the brickwork — these serve to draw the moisture out of the brick since they are more porous
- Chemical injection which is the most popular method in restoration schemes: holes are drilled 11.2 centimetres apart all the way round the house and fluid is pumped in and absorbed by the brickwork until it joins up, forming a moisture-proof seal.

The first two of the methods described above are expensive. If you are going to do the work yourself then chemical injection is the easiest method to administer. Alternatively, there are contractors who deal with damp coursing. This has the advantage that most of them give a 25-year guarantee and will often treat for rot and woodworm at the same time.

If you have a building society mortgage then damp proof work may be classed as an essential repair. In this case, the building society is likely to require that the work is covered by a formal guarantee. It is therefore unlikely that you would carry out the work yourself.

The roof

The roof should be inspected both internally and externally to see whether it needs repairing or replacing. If the property is old then replacement involving upgrading to modern standards is preferable in the long term. Beware of patching up the roof over a number of years only to find out at the end of this time that it needs fully replacing and that it would have been far easier — and cheaper — to have had this done initially. Repairing or replacing the roof is one of the most important jobs in a renovation programme, so a reliable contractor should be used. The work can take place at the same time as the damp coursing. The complexity of the work will range from repairs to pitched roofs involving slates and tiles to repairs to flat roofs covered in bituminous roofing felt. Costs will include the contractor's time, the cost of materials and that of removing the debris. Tiling is more expensive than roofing with slates.

The floor

The floor will have to be damp proof. If the existing floor is badly laid then it may be easiest to pull it up, lay a concrete slab of 20–25 centimetres deep on appropriate damp-proofing and finish it with a 5–7.5 centimetre screed of concrete. The simplest way of doing this is to pour concrete down a shute. Slab laying is best done with ready-mix whenever possible. Screeding can be done by hand-mixing or ready-mix. There are firms who will deliver the ingredients dry and mix it on site. It should be done after the slab is dry enough to walk on and after any gas, water and electricity services have been laid on the surface of the main slab.

If you want wooden floors but have difficulty in matching existing flooring, floorboards in good condition can be moved in from another room and lino or floor tiles laid in the rooms missing floorboards. This will allow you to have at least one room with the original wooden floors.

Structural changes and special features

Building an extension

The plans for the extension will have been drawn up by your architect or chartered surveyor. As the work progresses it will be checked regularly by the Building Control Officer. There are seven stages to the extension:

- Draining the site
- Pegging out and marking the foundations
- Excavating the foundations
- Shuttering and pouring concrete
- Building the shell
- Roofing in
- Completing internal work.

Special features

Restoration work can draw attention to interesting architectural features. You can repair or replace originals or substitute copies. For example, external mouldings can now be replaced by fibreglass ones so that it is hard to tell the difference between the two. These mouldings are factory-made and simply fitted in position with screws. Some interior mouldings are made from expanded polystyrene so they are also light and easy to fit.

Certain types of original skirting are irreplaceable. As with wooden floor tiles, you can carefully match good sections of existing skirting boards and move them from one room to another so that at least one room has the best-preserved features. Other skirting can then be replaced with ready-made, off-the-peg styles. Special types of skirting can be made up to match existing boards but this is very expensive.

If you are renovating an old property then period-style windows can be purchased that are in keeping with the house. Sash windows can be replaced. This is expensive but, as with replacements of all period features, gives the best result.

Plastering

Plaster only needs replacing where it has become detached from the walls or has been affected by winter-borne salts. Otherwise, it can be replaced by plastering a new layer over the top. You may need to consult a plasterer if the plaster is very old (upwards of 30 years) as it is then prone to crumble.

Heating

Gas central heating is by far the cheapest and most effective source of heating available at present. In addition to gas, there are several forms of heating to choose from such as electricity, solid fuel, oil, liquid gas etc. With all heating systems, you need to consider both installation and running costs.

Installation costs

Detailed estimates can be obtained for the installation costs of all different types of system using any fuel for any property. If you choose oil or liquid gas remember that a storage tank will be required and that there will have to be access for deliveries.

Running costs

Whichever fuel is used, running costs can be reduced if certain basic requirements are complied with. These are:

- Insulation of loft
- Cavity wall insulation (not recommended for timber-framed constructions)
- Double-glazing
- Draught-proofing
- Properly designed and installed systems
- Corrosion inhibitors
- Thermostatic radiator valves or similar controls
- Regular servicing
- Effective time and temperature controls
- Sensible room temperatures.

Whatever your requirements, renovation should incorporate features which will favourably influence running costs. It is also important to ensure that your property has sufficient ventilation to cope with the heating system you are considering; otherwise you may find that you have problems with condensation.

Electricity and water supplies

Replacing part of the electrical system can be as time-consuming as installing a completely new one. It is sure to be the case that the bit you do not repair will start to cause you problems. Complete replacement will give you the chance to rationalise the layout and bring all the parts up to a uniform standard. The same principle applies to water supplies and plumbing, including water storage tanks.

Decorating

This is the final and perhaps the most exciting part of the renovation process. Remember that, at worst, newly plastered walls may take up to six months to cure during which time they should not be papered.

So far we have assumed that everything has gone according to plan. Chapter 8 looks at what to do when things start to go wrong and examines the precautions that you can take to prevent this happening.

8

Insuring Your Property and What to Do if Things go Wrong

Insurance

Since your property is likely to be your most valuable asset, it is essential that it is suitably insured. Insurance falls into two main categories:

- Buildings insurance
- Contents insurance.

Insuring the building

Your building society or bank will insist that you take out an insurance policy to cover the structure of your property. This is called buildings insurance. Many building societies will help by sending you insurance quotations with your mortgage offer. While you are under no obligation to use the insurance company that the building society recommends, it will often be to your advantage to do so as the volume of business which they pass on may mean that they can offer you a policy which has been specially designed for their customers' needs. If you are buying a flat then buildings insurance is arranged by the managing agent and the cost shared by the residents.

The precise details of each policy will vary, so it is important to read all the relevant sections. Insurance is provided to cover the structure of your property in the event of disasters such as:

- Fire
- Storm
- Lightning
- Earthquake
- Flood
- Subsidence
- Explosion
- Collision by aircraft, vehicles, trains or animals.

Most policies *include* the:

- Structure
- Garages
- Permanent fixtures and fittings (eg toilet, bath),

but *exclude*:

- Fences
- Gates
- Hedges.

Most companies include provision for the cost of alternative accommodation for you and your family if the house becomes uninhabitable as the result of an insured risk. This is calculated as a percentage of the building sum insured. Look for a policy that also covers your legal liability towards third parties as a result of injuries to them or damage to their property. Most policies should include this. Such a policy would cover events such as slates falling off your roof and damaging your neighbour's house.

Some insurance policies have an 'excess' which is the amount you have to pay towards any claim that you make. If, for example, you make a claim for storm damage and the excess is £50, this amount would be deducted from your settlement cheque.

It may be better to look for a policy which does not have an excess. This sort of policy will evidently cost more so you must weigh up the advantages and disadvantages of doing this. All policies will include at least one excess — that relating to subsidence.

Pay careful attention to the sum for which the building is insured. It is easy to forget that this figure will need frequent updating. It is possible to have an insurance policy which is index-linked and your building society can provide details of this type of policy. If your cover is being arranged by your building society then the building society valuer will supply a figure which your insurance cover will be based upon. This figure is the maximum sum insured on your policy. If your property is not insured for the full reinstatement cost (ie the cost of rebuilding), the insurers may not pay your claim in full. Some building society policies include a rebuilding cost guarantee. Provided the building is insured for the full reinstatement value, as indicated by the building society valuer from the outset, and you continue to insure your property in line with index-linking, the guarantee will apply.

The cost of the reinstatement is not related to the market value — it can be much higher especially if non-standard building materials and methods of construction are used. These costs vary from region to region. A broad indication of your rebuilding costs can be obtained from the Building Cost Information Service of the Royal Institution of Chartered Surveyors (RICS).

If you need to make a claim you should act quickly. You will usually be asked to submit three quotations for repairs. If, having made a claim, you are dissatisfied with the settlement, you should take this up with your insurers. If you have still not received any satisfaction, you can contact the building society who arranged your cover. If all else fails, you could take your complaint to the Insurance Ombudsman's Bureau.

Insuring the contents

This is an optional policy although you are strongly urged to make sure that the contents of your home are adequately insured. Contents insurance covers a wide range of house contents and personal effects. Some policies will also cover personal possessions outside the home.

Certain items, for example jewellery, musical instruments and bicycles, may be covered up to a particular limit. Many policies also provide additional cover while the owner is temporarily absent from the property.

All policies vary so you need to choose the one that best suits your needs. If, for example, all your family use bicycles then it is advisable to choose a policy which includes bicycles as part of the standard cover. Some policies include accidental damage to your contents and personal effects.

Calculating the value of the contents of your house or flat needs careful thought. If you insure it for too little your claims may not be met in full. Most policies provide charts showing you how to calculate the value of your house contents. It is easy to forget to add in the cost of the carpet or to undervalue the furniture. It is often surprising just how high the insured figure is. With some building society policies it is not necessary to calculate the sum insured providing you are sure that it does not exceed a set figure which is usually a fixed percentage of the reinstatement value.

As with building insurance, you can elect to have your policy index-linked. Your building society will be able to advise you on this.

All insurance companies calculate the premium according to the risk involved. This means that you may pay a higher premium for living in a 'high risk' area such as an inner city area. You could find yourself in a high risk area on one company's charts but not on another's, and choosing the latter could save you some money.

It is important to note that buildings and contents insurance can be combined in one insurance policy (but obviously not if you live in a flat, for the reasons stated above). You can take out such a policy through your insurance company or via your building society.

Insuring your home while the building work is going on

When building work occurs, the risk of damage to your property increases and you must make sure that you have adequate insurance cover. Your building society will be able to advise you on this. In order to arrange suitable cover, the insurance company will require certain details, for example:

- Whether you are likely to be living in the property while restoration work is carried out; if not, for how long the property is likely to remain unoccupied
- Whether the property will be furnished or unfurnished
- Who will carry out the restoration work planned
- The scale of the work and the possible contract value
- Whether any temporary structure such as scaffolding or a porta-cabin has been erected
- When the work is scheduled to start and finish.

The types of risk to which you may be vulnerable during the building work include:

- Security threats, eg materials stolen from the site
- Accidental damage, eg putting your foot through the ceiling while insulating your loft
- Possible negligence, eg setting the house on fire.

It is important to check exactly what your policy covers. Some policies, for example, may exclude accidental damage.

If you are hiring a professional or a builder you must ascertain, at the outset, who is responsible for what. Most standard forms of contract for building work contain a section regarding insurance that puts responsibility on both the builder and the customer. You must therefore ask to see proof that the people you employ are adequately covered. It is standard practice for the householder to extend his building insurance to cover the existing building, the new structure, materials and plant on site for the period of the contract. You should confirm in writing, to your builder or professional, who is responsible for what. Contracts can often be technical; if you have any problem understanding the terms you could ask your solicitor for assistance.

If the property is to be left unoccupied for any period of time then this will affect your cover. Your building society can advise you on this and arrange for extra cover when required, although you will naturally have to pay a premium for this.

What to do if things go wrong and where to get help

For quick, objective advice you can go to your local Trading Standards (or Consumer Protection) Department, the Citizens' Advice Bureau or the Consumer Advice Centre.

Disputes with professionals

If you have employed a professional to take charge of all or some of the building work and are not happy with his performance then there are a number of things that you can do. The first is to try to sort the matter out informally — it may be that there has been a simple misunderstanding. If you have no joy then you can refer the matter to his professional institution or association.

The professional institutions have codes of conduct that their members must abide by and these are set out in Chapter 9. You should contact the secretary of the institution to which your professional belongs. Ask for details of the code of conduct. You may find that this covers only fraud and other serious misconduct but not incompetence or negligence.

If your dispute is over fees then go back to your original contract which should include the fee that you agreed to pay. RIBA and RICS handle disputes over fees and the cases that cannot be resolved in this way are referred to arbitration. Again you need to check that your original contract allows for arbitration. The standard contracts of many organisations include an arbitration clause. No legal costs are incurred in this relatively informal way of resolving disputes.

Before going on to the next stage — legal action — you should consult a solicitor. Most professionals will have indemnity cover to protect them against such claims but this works to your advantage as, if you win, you can be assured of receiving the money. An out-of-court settlement may be suggested and you are often advised to take this, especially if your case is likely to be difficult to prove in court.

Disputes with builders

For independent advice, go to the Citizens' Advice Bureau (CAB). Another source of information is your local Trading Standards Office. You could also consult a professional for his advice on the dispute. Always go back to the original contract to check what it was that you asked to be done. If you have been keeping proper control of the works programme then you will also have a note of any extra work, variations, delays etc with the appropriate dates. The dispute should be referred to the trade association to which the builder belongs, for example the Federation of Master Builders. The institutions and associations and their codes of practice are discussed in Chapter 9.

Whether the dispute is with a professional or your builder, you can always go back to your building society for advice. You can rest assured that they will have encountered your problem, or a very similar one, before and will be able to point you in the right direction for help. It may be depressing when things go wrong but it is always encouraging to hear that someone else has had similar problems and resolved them.

How to discharge workers if you are dissatisfied with their performance

If you are contemplating discharging someone then, to protect yourself, you must adhere to certain procedures. This will cover you should the case ever go to court. You should warn the builder if you are not happy with his work. You must put it in writing that you may cancel his contract and find a replacement. Grounds for complaint could be that your builder:

- Fails to keep to an agreed schedule and does not finish on time
- Disappears completely or tries to carry out work for a number of different parties to the satisfaction of no-one (except perhaps himself)
- Fails to rectify earlier mistakes
- Fails to return to correct any defects that have occurred within the defects liability period
- Goes bankrupt.

You should follow this procedure:

- Meet with the builder, tell him what is wrong (and later put this in writing) and find out what action he intends to take and when
- Keep a note of the dates and times of your meetings or of the number of times you tried unsuccessfully to make contact
- Write a letter outlining the sequence of events and state what action you require the builder to take. State that the builder has 14 working days to carry out the work or you will engage another builder and charge this to your original builder. Send the letter by recorded delivery
- If after 14 days you still have not heard anything then write another letter reiterating the fact that you are about to employ someone else as he is now in breach of contract. State your intention to pay him only for the work he has completed and not for the full contract sum
- Inform the builder that he should collect his equipment.

If the builder goes bankrupt or dies the procedure is more complicated and you should take legal advice.

If you are forced to take on a second builder (ie as a replacement) then again you must protect yourself so that you cannot be sued for breach of contract by your original builder. The second builder must only carry out work described in the original contract. It is no good getting him to mend the fence while he is there if you have not already asked for this to be done by the first builder. You must inform the second builder why he is being hired. Quotes should be obtained from at least two builders so that you cannot be accused of hiring someone who is too expensive.

You must work out as accurately as possible how much the first builder is owed. If the work by the second builder comes to more than the difference between the full contract sum and what you paid the first builder then you can charge the first builder for this additional sum.

Always consult a solicitor before embarking on legal action. If the original builder is a member of the Building Employers Confederation (BEC) or the Federation of Master Builders and was doing the work under their guarantee or warranty scheme then check the scheme's requirements before engaging a second builder. This is so that you can benefit from the payment of the scheme towards any costs in excess of the original contract sum. For details of the BEC guarantee scheme contact the BEC Building Trust, a subsidiary of the BEC.

Each of the trade and professional bodies will provide details of their guarantee schemes. For example, if your enquiry is about roofing then contact the National Federation of Roofing Contractors.

What to do in emergencies and how to avoid them

The best way of dealing with emergencies is to avoid them! Although there are certain precautions that you can take, there will usually be something that goes wrong — for example a leaking roof. Tips for avoiding disasters include making sure that:

- Pipes are lagged so that they are less likely to burst during a cold spell
- Gutters and drains are kept clear of obstructions
- The roof is regularly checked for any missing tiles
- Repairs are carried out immediately and not left until emergency action is needed
- You know where all the stopcocks/valves are so that you can turn off the water immediately
- Water heaters, gas fires and other gas appliances are regularly serviced — at least once a year
- Frequent checks are made on the need for rewiring.

If, despite the above precautions, an emergency occurs, the best advice is to try to stay calm as you will then be more effective. The first step is to assess the nature of the problem and whether it needs immediate attention. If you call out an electrician or plumber out of usual working hours then his services will be much more expensive. If your property is being damaged or the ceiling is liable to fall in if the leak is not attended to immediately, then of course you must take swift action.

Do not panic or you will forget the vital questions that you need to ask the plumber. If possible, do not ring the first number that you find in *Yellow Pages* that offers a 24-hour service. Get a couple of alternative quotes and try to ascertain whether you will be paying:

- VAT
- A standard call-out charge
- An extra charge for materials.

If your home is collapsing around you, of course, you will not have the luxury of following these procedures. That is why it is so useful to have prepared the way in advance.

Rather than waiting for the emergency to occur and then wondering what you are going to do, it would be useful to have a list of tradesmen's quotes to hand. If you have taken the trouble to ask them about their charges beforehand then you need only select a candidate from your list. The vital issues will be whether they are available outside office hours and how quickly they can respond to an emergency call.

In the next chapter details are given of the various professional and trade associations and the codes of practice to which their members are subjected. It examines the extent to which you are protected if you employ someone who is a member of a particular association.

9
Membership of Professional and Trade Associations

Professional and trade associations exist primarily to promote the interests of their members. Because of this, it is to their advantage to prevent disreputable practice from damaging the good name of that industry. That is why some of the associations have drawn up customer protection policies. It is worth hiring a professional or a builder who is affiliated to one of the main bodies as he will then have some accountability should things go wrong. It must be remembered, however, that many of the associations do not have the facility to cope with serious disputes. Names and addresses of professional and trade associations can be found in the Useful Addresses section at the end of this book. In this chapter, some of the more commonly encountered organisations are described together with brief details of their codes of practice and guarantee schemes. For more details it is best to write to the association.

Architects

As was mentioned in Chapter 5, only professionally qualified people are allowed to call themselves architects. The professional institution to which many belong is the *Royal Institute of British Architects* (RIBA).

The Scottish equivalent is the *Royal Incorporation of Architects in Scotland* (RIAS).

The professional conduct committee of RIBA can handle complaints that relate to:

- Dishonesty or lack of integrity
- Improper conduct of a client's affairs
- Abuse of confidentiality
- Allowing other interests to conflict with a client's interests
- Improperly obtaining commissions

RIAS will deal with complaints that relate to:

- Disgraceful conduct
- Conflict of interest
- Proceeding without a client's permission
- Failure to keep within the budget
- Failure to adhere to the procedures laid down in the conditions of appointment.

Either institution can provide more detailed information on the specific details of their codes of conduct.

Builders

The building industry has trade organisations which set standards for their members. Recently, they have broadened their role to offer 'guarantee schemes'. Guarantee or warranty schemes are particularly useful if the builder goes bankrupt or dies.

Look for builders who can provide evidence that they are members of the *Building Employers' Confederation* (BEC), the *Federation of Master Builders* (FMB) or the *Chartered Institute of Building* (CIOB), as all these organisations provide guarantee schemes.

The BEC guarantee scheme

This scheme is operated by the *BEC Building Trust*, part of the BEC. Currently it covers jobs worth between £5000 and £35,000 involving all normal building and home improvement works. The scheme covers the following contingencies:

- Damage of goods and materials, from day one of the work, is covered by insurance
- A replacement BEC member will be provided if the first builder does not finish the work
- Any faults which are discovered within the defects liability period (within six months of the original work having been completed) will be rectified by the builder
- Any 'structural' defect that occurs within a further two years will be put right
- A replacement BEC builder will be provided if the first one goes out of business. If the work then costs more than the original agreed sum then the BEC will pay up to a maximum of £5000 plus VAT for additional costs
- In the case of a dispute, the BEC will appoint an independent, professionally qualified adviser.

Your builder can organise the above scheme for you. The work must be carried out under a formal written contract — a special 'guarantee scheme' contract — approved by the *Office of Fair Trading* (OFT). The charge for this scheme is 1 per cent of the contract sum (minimum £20).

National Register of Warranted Builders

This warranty scheme is operated by the FMB. It is important to note that just because a builder is a member of the Federation this does not mean that he is part of the scheme. The warranty scheme covers any type of work up to the value of £50,000 including VAT. It must be entered into before any work has begun. The warranty provides the following:

- A guarantee that for up to two years after the work is completed any defects through faulty workmanship or materials reported in writing to the Federation register will, if agreed with, be rectified at no extra cost to the customer
- If the builder goes out of business or dies a replacement builder will be found to finish the work or put right any defects. The warranty covers extra work of up to £8000 if the work costs more than the original sum
- Provision of a conciliation or arbitration service in the case of a dispute. If proved right, the registration board will pay the reasonable cost of the works which another builder will then undertake.

The scheme costs 1 per cent of the contract sum. The minimum fee is £5.

Electricians

There are two regulatory bodies which set standards for electrical work that is carried out in your house. These are the *National Inspection Council for Electrical Installation Contracting* (NICEIC) and the *Electrical Contractors' Association* (ECA). The former is an independent consumer safety body which is there to protect the users of electrical installations. The NICEIC has a list of over 11,000 members who are approved electrical contractors. Their work must conform to the IEE (Institution of Electrical Engineers) wiring regulations and related BSI (British Standards Institution) codes of practice. Approved contractors are inspected regularly to make sure that they are maintaining the required standards of workmanship and safety.

The ECA is the trade association for the electrical contracting industry. Employees of member firms must be fully trained and qualified. The ECA issues a list of members which can be obtained by writing to them. Their customers are offered certain safeguards and guarantees which include:

- A replacement worker to rectify poor or unfinished work at no extra cost to the customer.

The *Electrical Contractors' Association of Scotland* (ECA of S) also has a code of good practice. If the ECA of S is to intervene in a case of complaint then it must receive this complaint in writing within 12 months of the work being carried out.

Engineers

There are many different types of engineer but only those most likely to be encountered during the course of building work on the home are mentioned here. The professional body for structural engineers is the *Institution of Structural Engineers*. The designatory letters for chartered structural engineer members are CEng.MIStructE or CEng.FIStructE; for technician members TEng.AMIStructE. You are likely to use a structural engineer only if you need to make a large hole in a wall or if the foundations or cavity wall ties of your property have failed.

You may need a heating engineer if you are thinking of installing a pressurised (unvented) domestic water system. These are covered by British Standards. The *British Board of Agrément* has certification for unvented hot water storage systems and an approved system for installers.

Organisations covering heating work are the *Heating and Ventilating Contractors' Association* (HVCA), the *National Association of Plumbing, Heating and Mechanical Services Contractors*, the *Scottish and Northern Ireland Plumbing Employers' Federation* and the *Institute of Plumbing*.

Members of the HVCA must agree to install a variety of systems and to offer the HVCA 'double' guarantee on new domestic central heating installations. This lasts for a year and means that:

- The central heating system must perform in accordance with the specifications
- Safety standards are adhered to
- Standards are observed for the quality of design, workmanship and materials.

The HVCA has a complaints procedure. If the first HVCA member fails to complete the work satisfactorily another member will be commissioned at no extra cost to the customer. There is also a code of practice applying to all work not covered by the double guarantee. This usually covers repairs, servicing and maintenance of an existing system or equipment. The code provides guidance on:

- Standards of workmanship and materials
- Costs
- Payment terms
- Settlement of disputes.

An extended warranty scheme is also on offer. This provides insurance for three to five years (inclusive of the one-year guarantee period) on payment of a single premium. An application form and details can be obtained from the HCVA.

Glazing contractors

The double glazing industry is carefully monitored by the Office of Fair Trading. The main association for double glazing companies is the

Glass and Glazing Federation (GGF). The GGF has drawn up a code of practice in association with the OFT to which all members must conform. This covers all the stages from advertising and selling the product to after-sales service and complaints.

It is usual to pay a deposit of between 10 and 25 per cent of the contract price. The GGF will indemnify you so that even if the firm you are dealing with goes bust you will not lose your deposit. The GGF will arrange for someone else to do the work at a 'fair market rate'.

An arbitration scheme exists to handle disputes and has been drawn up in association with the *Chartered Institute of Arbitrators*. This is based on written submissions and the Institute undertakes to reach a decision within three months of the original referral. A registration fee of £20–30 is payable by the customer.

Insulation contractors

The *National Association of Loft Insulation Contractors* deals primarily with loft insulation. There is a code of practice for members and a warranty which obliges a member to:

- Investigate any complaints a customer may have
- Rectify any defects arising from faulty materials or workmanship provided that the firm is notified in writing within six months of the completion date.

An arbitration scheme has been set up to handle disputes.

The *External Wall Insulation Association* (EWIA) deals with cladding a building in order to insulate and renovate the external walls. Members are specialist designers and contractors. A technical standard exists in the form of a detailed specification covering system certification, testing procedures, component parts and performance criteria.

For cavity wall insulation look for members of the *National Cavity Insulation Association* (NCIA). There is an NCIA code of practice, which governs adherence to minimum technical standards and the imparting of misleading information. There is also a customer protection plan which allows the Association to mediate in the case of disputes.

Other associations such as the *Cavity Foam Bureau* and the *Draught Proofing Advisory Association Ltd* exist to cover the cavity foam insulation industry and the draught proofing industry respectively. Both can be contacted for details of their codes of practice.

Plumbers

Anyone can set himself up as a plumber or plumbing contractor, so it is imperative that you choose a member of a trade association or at least find out if your 'plumber' has any training qualifications.

The *Institute of Plumbing* is registered as a charity not a trade association. Registered plumbers, about 11,000 at present, are monitored under the BSI's Public Register Inspection Maintenance Assessment scheme (PRIMA). The Institute does not intervene in contractual disputes and all it can do is strike someone off the register.

There are other composite bodies which cover the heating industry, such as the *National Association of Plumbing, Heating and Mechanical Services Contractors* (already mentioned) and the *Scottish and Northern Ireland Plumbing Employers' Federation*. Members are vetted before they are allowed to register. The associations have a code of practice approved by the OFT which covers:

- A list of 'fair and reasonable conditions between firms and customers'
- Principles for dealing with customers' complaints.

Roofing contractors

The trade association for firms primarily involved with roofing operations is the *National Federation of Roofing Contractors* (NFRC). Contractors have to satisfy the Federation's standards before they are allowed to join. These include:

- Having a responsible trading record for a minimum of two or three years
- Inspection of work in progress and work recently completed
- Inspection of premises and stock yard.

Workmanship must comply with BSI codes of practice. The NFRC has an insurance-backed guarantee scheme to cover for ten years so that even if the original contractor has disappeared work can still be carried out under guarantee.

Surveyors (chartered)

The Professional Practice Department of the *Royal Institution of Chartered Surveyors* (RICS) will investigate complaints against chartered surveyors if they relate to:

- Inexplicable delays in dealing with clients' affairs
- Failure to reply to letters
- Disclosure of confidential information
- Failure to disclose a conflict between a client's interests and that of the surveyor
- Dishonesty.

The RICS offers a chartered surveyors' arbitration scheme which is run independently by the *Chartered Institute of Arbitrators*. This scheme operates at present in England and Wales but not yet in Scotland. Details are available from the RICS Professional Practice Department or from the Chartered Institute of Arbitrators. Each party pays a registration fee plus VAT. As with all formal arbitration schemes, the arbitrator's decision is final. The surveyor cannot then be sued in court on the same charge.

• • • • •

The above list is by no means exhaustive. Before employing any professional, builder or contractor it is prudent to consult a trade or professional body for a recommendation or to find out about their code of practice. If you have planned and supervised the work efficiently yourself then you are less likely to need to have recourse to an institution or association. They should be looked on as a last resort and not as a safeguard for sloppiness on your part. Apart from this, going to arbitration or litigation may eventually become more of a nightmare in the long term than settling with the builder informally.

Postscript: Ten Golden Rules for the House Restorer

1. *Finances* — find out BEFORE you look for a new home how much you can afford to borrow to buy and restore the property.
2. *Choosing a home* — carefully consider your basic requirements and work out how much work needs to be done to restore the property and what this will cost. Remember to allow for unexpected costs.
3. *Local authority approval* — find out BEFORE you buy the house whether you need planning permission for the work you intend to carry out. Find out if you will need building regulations approval and whether or not you are eligible for a grant towards the work.
4. *Making the purchase* — try to remain calm, do not let anyone rush you, and communicate regularly with your solicitor.
5. *Managing the works programme* — if the alterations are extensive and complex then seek the help of a professional. If you decide to handle the day-to-day running of the site make sure that every stage is carefully planned. Obtain quotations from at least three firms if you hire builders or contractors.
6. *Your contract with a firm* — make sure the contract is in writing and gives full details of prices, cancellation rights, guarantees, and when the work is to start and finish. Check whether subcontractors will be used and, if so, who is liable if things go wrong.
7. *Payment* — do not pay builders BEFORE they start work. Keep a record of every payment you make including that for any 'extra work'. Keep all your invoices and show these to your building society if you have opted for a house restoration mortgage.
8. *Insurance* — make sure that you have taken out insurance to cover the building work and that this is extended if the work goes on longer than anticipated.
9. *If things go wrong* — seek impartial advice from the local Trading Standards Department, Citizens' Advice Bureau or Consumer Advice Centre. In an emergency, stay calm, evaluate the extent of the damage and only call an expert if you really need to.
10. *Throughout the purchase and restoration programme* — retain a sense of humour at all times, keep calm and try not to panic.

Appendix: British Standards

Almost every building operation is governed by a set standard. The British Standards Institution (BSI) — the national standards organisation — issues British standards. These define the type and quality of materials. Most building materials and components have a 'BS' number. The BSI also publish Codes of Practice describing how the various materials should be combined to produce work of a certain quality.

The BSI 'kitemark' is a registered certification trademark which indicates that the BSI have issued a licence to the manufacturer, after independent tests have been carried out to ensure that the product complies with British Standards.

Useful Names and Addresses

Architects' Registration Council
73 Hallam Street
London W1N 6EE
01-580 5861

Association of British Insurers
Aldermary House
Queen Street
London EC4N 1TT
01-248 4477

Association of Licensed Conveyancers
200–201 High Street
Exeter EX4 3EB

BEC Building Trust
18 Mansfield Street
London W1M 9FG
01-580 6306

British Board of Agrément
PO Box 195
Bucknalls Lane
Garston
Watford
Herts WD2 7NG
0923 670844

British Chemical Damp Course Association
16a Whitchurch Road
Pangbourne
Berks RG8 7BP

British Institute of Architectural Technicians
397 City Road
London EC1V 1NE
01-278 2206

British Insurance Brokers' Association (BIBA)
BIBA House
14 Bevis Marks
London EC3N 7AT
01-623 9043

British Safety Council
62 Chancellors Road
London W6 9RS
01-741 1231

British Standards Institution
2 Park Street
London W1A 2BS
01-629 9000

British Wood Preserving Association
6 The Office Village
4 Romford Road
London E15 4EA
01-519 2588

Building Centres
26 Store Street
London WC1E 7BT
01-637 1022
35 King Street
Bristol BS1 4DZ
0272 260264
113–115 Portland Street
Manchester M1 6FB
061-236 9802
131 West Nile Street
Glasgow G1 2RX
041-333 9701

Building Employers Confederation
82 New Cavendish Street
London W1M 8AD
01-580 5588

Building Research Establishment
Bucknalls Lane
Garston
Watford
Herts WD2 7JR
0923 894040

Cavity Foam Bureau
PO Box 79
Oldbury
Warley
West Midlands B69 4PW
021-544 4949

Chartered Institute of Arbitrators
International Arbitration Centre
75 Cannon Street
London EC4N 5BH
01-236 8761

Chartered Institute of Building
Englemere
Kings Ride
Ascot
Berks SL5 8BJ
0990 23355

Consumers Association
14 Buckingham Street
London WC2N 6DF
01-839 1222

Corporation of Insurance and Financial Advisers (CIFA)
6–7 Leapale Road
Guildford
Surrey GU1 4JX

Council of Licensed Conveyancers
Golden Cross House
Duncannon Street
London WC2N 4JF
01-210 4603

Department of the Environment (Housing)
Victoria Road
Ruislip
Middlesex HA4 0NZ

Draught Proofing Advisory Association Ltd
PO Box 12
Haslemere
Surrey GU27 3AN
0428 54011

Electrical Contractors' Association
ESCA House
34 Palace Court
London W2 4HY
01-229 1266

Electrical Contractors' Association of Scotland
23 Heriot Row
Edinburgh EH3 6EW
031-225 7221

English Heritage
Fortress House
23 Savile Row
London W1X 2HE
01-734 6010

External Wall Insulation Association
PO Box 12
Haslemere
Surrey GU27 3AN
0428 54011

The Faculty of Architects and Surveyors
15 St Mary Street
Chippenham
Wiltshire SN15 3JN

Federation of Master Builders
Gordon Fisher House
33 John Street
London WC1N 2BB
01-242 7583

Glass and Glazing Federation
44–48 Borough High Street
London SE1 1XB
01-403 7177

Guarantee Protection Trust
PO Box 77
27 London Road
High Wycombe
Bucks HP11 1BW
0494 447049

Guild of Master Craftsmen
166 High Street
Lewes
East Sussex BN7 1XU
0273 478449

Health and Safety Commission
Regina House
259 Old Marylebone Road
London NW1 5RR
01-723 1262

Health and Safety Executive
25 Chapel Street
London NW1 5DT
01-262 3277

Heating and Ventilating Contractors' Association
ESCA House
34 Palace Court
London W2 4JG
01-229 2488
23 Heriot Row
Edinburgh EH3 6EW
031-225 8212

Historic Buildings Bureau for Scotland
New St Andrews House
St James Centre
Edinburgh EH1 3SZ

Historic Buildings Company
PO Box 150
Chobham
Surrey GU24 8JD

The Incorporated Association of Architects and Surveyors
Jubilee House
Billing Brook Road
Weston Favell
Northampton NN3 4NW
0604 404121

The Incorporated Society of Valuers and Auctioneers
3 Cadogan Gate
London SW1X 0AS
01-235 2282

Institute of Building Control
21 High Street
Ewell
Epsom
Surrey KT17 1SB
01-393 6860

Institute of Plumbing
64 Station Lane
Hornchurch
Essex RM12 6NB
04024 72791

Institute of Wood Science
Stocking Lane
Hughenden Valley
High Wycombe
Bucks HP14 4NU
0240 245374

Institution of Electrical Engineers
Savoy Place
London WC2R 0BL
01-240 1871

Institution of Structural Engineers
11 Upper Belgrave Street
London SW1X 8BH
01-235 4535

The Insurance Ombudsman
31 Southampton Row
London WC1B 5HJ
01-242 8613

Kitchen Specialists Association
8 St Bernard's Crescent
Edinburgh EH4 1NP
031-332 8884

Law Commission
Conquest House
37 St John Street
London WC1N 2BQ
01-242 0861

The Law Society
113 Chancery Lane
London WC2A 1PL
01-242 1222

Law Society of Scotland
26 Drumsheugh Gardens
Edinburgh EH3 7YR
031-226 7411

Mastic Asphalt Council and Employers Federation
24 Weymouth Street
London W1N 3FA
01-436 0102

The National Association of Conveyancers
2–4 Chichester Rents
Chancery Lane
London WC2A 1EJ
01-405 8582

The National Association of Estate Agents
Arbon House
21 Jury Street
Warwick CV34 4EH
0926 496800

National Association of Loft Insulation Contractors
PO Box 12
Haslemere
Surrey GU27 3AN
0428 54011

National Association of Plumbing, Heating and Mechanical Services Contractors
6 Gate Street
London WC2A 3HX
01-405 2678

National Cavity Insulation Association
PO Box 12
Haslemere
Surrey GU27 3AN
0428 54011

National Federation of Building Trade Employees
82 New Cavendish Street
London W1M 8AD
01-580 5588

National Federation of Roofing Contractors
24 Weymouth Street
London W1N 3FA
01-436 0387

National Home Improvement Council
26 Store Street
London WC1E 7BT
01-636 2562

National House Building Council
Buildmark House
Chiltern Avenue
Amersham
Bucks HP6 5AP

National Inspection Council for Electrical Installation Contracting
Vintage House
36–37 Albert Embankment
London SE1 7UJ
01-582 7746

Office of Fair Trading
Chancery House
Chancery Lane
London WC2A 1SP
01-242 2858

RIBA Publications
33 Mooreland Street
London EC1V 8BB
01-251 0791

RICS Publications Department
Norden House
Basingstoke
Hants FG21 2HN
0256 55234

Royal Incorporation of Architects in Scotland
15 Rutland Square
Edinburgh EH1 2BE
031-229 7205

Royal Institute of British Architects
66 Portland Place
London W1N 4AD
01-580 5533

Royal Institution of Chartered Surveyors
12 Great George Street
London SW1P 3AD
01-222 7000
9 Manor Place
Edinburgh EH3 7DN
031-225 7078

Royal Society of Ulster Architects
2 Mount Charles
Belfast BT7 1NZ
0232 323760

Royal Town Planning Institute
26 Portland Place
London W1N 4BE
01-636 9107
15 Rutland Square
Edinburgh EH1 2BE
031-337 3423

Save Britain's Heritage
68 Battersea High Street
London SW11 3HX
01-228 3336
New St Andrews House
St James Centre
Edinburgh EH1 3SZ

Scottish Building Employers Federation
13 Woodside Crescent
Glasgow G3 7UP
041-332 7144

Scottish and Northern Ireland Plumbing Employers' Federation
2 Walker Street
Edinburgh EH3 7LB
031-225 2255

Society for the Protection of Ancient Buildings
37 Spital Square
London E1 6DY
01-377 1644

Society of Architects in Wales
75a Llandennis Road
Rhydypennau
Cardiff CF2 6EE
0222 762215

Society of Surveying Technicians
Drayton House
30 Gordon Street
London WC1H 0BH
01-388 8008

Solid Fuel Advisory Service
Hobart House
Grosvenor Place
London SW1X 7AW
01-235 2020

Further Reading

Buying and selling houses

Buying and Renovating Houses for Profit, K Ludman and R D Buchanan (Kogan Page)
Buying and Selling a House or Flat, H Green (Kogan Page)
Do It Yourself Conveyancing, R T Steele (David and Charles)
The Legal Side of Buying a House (Consumers' Association)

Grants

Home Improvement Grants: A Guide For Home Owners, Landlords, and Tenants, Department of the Environment, Housing Booklet No 14 (HMSO)

The building regulations

The Building Regulations (HMSO)
The Building Regulations Explained and Illustrated, W S Whyte and V Powell-Smith (Collins)
Guide to the Building Regulations 1985, A J Elder (Architectural Press)

General practical information

Alteration or Conversion of Houses, J F Garner (Longman)
Bazaar Property Doctor, I Morris (BBC Books)
Brickwork Repair and Restoration, W G Nash (Attic)
The Complete Home Carpenter (Orbis)
A Concise Building Encyclopaedia, ed. T Corkhill (Pitman)
Getting Work Done on your House, Which? Books (Hodder & Stoughton)
Home Improvement Price Guide, B Spain and L Morley (Spon)
House and Cottage Conversion: Guide to the Dos and Don'ts, H Lander (Acanthus Books)
House and Cottage Interiors: Dos and Don'ts of, H Lander (Acanthus Books)

The House Restorer's Guide, H Lander (David and Charles)
How to Restore and Improve Your Victorian House, A Johnson (David and Charles)
Landscaping (Time Life Books)
Repairing Houses, T James (Sphere)
Running Your Own Building Business, K Ludman (Kogan Page)
The Sunday Times Book of Do-It-Yourself (Sphere)
Surveying for Home-Buyers, D Broughton and J Dryborough (Penguin)

Heating

Do Your Own Central Heating, T Crabtree (Foulsham)

Layout and decor

The House Book, T Conran (Mitchell Beazley)

Architectural styles and historical information

The English Country Cottage, R J Brown (Robert Hale/Hamlyn)
English Farmhouses, R J Brown (Robert Hale/Hamlyn)
How Old is Your House? P Cunnington (Collins)
The Smaller English House: Its History and Development, L F Cave (Robert Hale)
Timber-Framed Buildings of England, R J Brown (Robert Hale)
The Windmills of Hampshire, A Triggs (Milestone)

Index

Index